POCKET FULL
OF POESY

A COLLECTION OF POEMS
BY M. HILL

MW00425979

Also by M. Hill

The Ones That Got Away ~ A Dating Memoir

Reading this book was just like eating salted peanuts. Once I started, I could not stop. M. Hill has managed to put into words what many women have personally experienced. Although she tells of her stories in a funny way, you know they are built on real emotions that at the time were not so funny: 'I'm embarrassed to admit it, but for a long while I half expected to find him chivalrously showing up at my house again—but he never did.' That line just got me, but overall, fun, fun, fun. Pass the peanuts... ~ P. Wilco, B&N Reviewer

This book cracked me up. I loved the humor. As a great observer of human behavior, this book gave me fascinating insights into both the male and female capricious conundrums of dating. Most appealing though was the honesty with which the author divulged her inner most emotions at the many highs and lows. This book holds many insights apart from being a darn good read. ~ Safari-Rob, B&N Reviewer

I kept thinking of the movie *Bridget Jones's Diary* as I devoured this book. Hill's adventures in dating kept me reading, laughing, and turning yet one more page to find out what could possibly happen next. I was hooked from the beginning... A look at dating quite unlike any other book you've read. ~ J.L.S., Amazon Reviewer

Unconditional ~ A Story of Love and Loss

Learn about what true love means, and how to live a meaningful life. When reading this excellent book you feel as if the author is sitting right next to you at a coffee shop and telling the story, a universal one! Highly entertaining and enlightening! ~ Fran K., Amazon Reviewer

Very well written! Emotional and sad, but also filled with HOPE and a bit of humor. This will surely bring comfort to believers who read this. ~ Michael S., Amazon Reviewer

A wonderful heartfelt book that pulls you into the story of her interactions with her parents through life phases of living, loving and dying. Really captures the intimacy and closeness of sharing that journey at life's end. Loved it. ~ Linda S., Amazon Reviewer

The Butterscotch Chronicles ~ An Anecdotal Look at Aging

This 2020 Bronze recipient in the Memoir/Biography category for the Feathered Quill Book Awards garnered the following judges' comments:

"Hysterical, self-deprecating humor. This is a way to look at life as only a person who is aging can."

"Even when times are tough, this is a book that would make everyone smile."

"Erma Bombeck and her titles always made me laugh when she wrote about everything from motherhood to family—Hill's voice is as great as hers."

Other comments:

"M. Hill's book was many things to me: funny, witty, relatable. Most importantly it was "REAL." Hill has a way of connecting with her readers that draws them in, and makes them feel like she is telling the story in that moment." ~ Jenna Urban, Goodreads Reviewer

"Life's real beauty exposed. You may have never read a book like this. Laughed as the precious moments are reflected on in a writing style that compounds the feelings we all share. Few people would write this, all people know it." ~ Mark R. Amo, Amazon Reviewer

Pocket Full of Poesy

A Collection of Poems
by M. Hill

Honeybee Publishing Company

Honeybee Publishing Company
Scottsdale, AZ 85262

Copyright ©2020, Honeybee Publishing Company
All rights reserved.

LCCN 2020911485
Print ISBN 978-0-9817500-6-4
Ebook ISBN 978-0-9817500-7-1
Copyright information available upon request.

Cover Design: J. L. Saloff and Manuta/iStockPhoto
Interior Design: J. L. Saloff
Typography: Garamond Premier Pro, Copperplate

Except in the United States of America, this book is sold subject to the
condition that it shall not, by way of trade or otherwise, be lent, resold,
hired out, or otherwise circulated without the publisher's prior consent
in any form of binding or cover other than that in which it is published
and without a similar condition including this condition being imposed
on the subsequent purchaser.

The scanning, uploading and distribution of this book via the Internet
or via any other means without permission of the publisher is illegal and
punishable by law. Please purchase only authorized electronic editions,
and do not participate in or encourage electronic piracy of copyrighted
materials. Your support of the author's rights is appreciated.

v. 1.01
First Edition, 2020
Printed on acid free paper.

For creative types everywhere...
let your lights shine!

ACKNOWLEDGMENTS

It's a collaborative process crafting a book.
I don't do it alone, so please take a look.

Those who assist me make the whole matter fun;
Without their help, it couldn't be done.

Where grammar's concerned, Sharon's first-rate;
There isn't a thing she can't punctuate.

Patient and kind, Jamie never says, "nay."
She's always willing to jump into the fray—

Using ideas that were lodged in my mind,
She achieved perfection with the cover design!

Whatever it takes to be supportive of me,
She's about as steadfast as my beloved JC.

CONTENTS ∼

∼∋

INTRODUCTION ∼

My name is Melissa, but most people call me Missy. Throughout my years I've tried, somewhat, to shake this moniker, but to no avail. The reason I say somewhat is because I never tried to shake it within my own family. To be quite frank, I preferred it within my family. As is often the case, when my full name was used, I was generally in trouble for some reason or another; and when my full name was used accompanied by my middle name, well, then there wasn't any question—I knew the proverbial you-know-what was hitting the fan.

I am a middle child. Even though my parents divorced when I was young and both remarried—providing me a variety of step and half siblings—I am originally a middle child. The older sibling is my sister Linda, who was also called Missy as a toddler. I think it's pretty common for toddler girls to be called Missy, but when I burst onto the scene a few years later, as the name transferred to me, she ceased to be called Missy, and just like that, everyone called her Linda—well, everyone apart from my grandfather, who called her Cocoa-marsh, that is. Then, before I was two years old, my brother Tim was born. Naturally, being a boy, the name Missy did not transfer to him and, as such, it has stuck with me. My mother also used to call me Missy Poodle, so I suppose I should be grateful *that* didn't stick—although I did like it when she called me that. Anyway, as a middle child, I did sometimes feel lost in the shuffle and often functioned in my own little world. This, you will see, is relevant.

I'm what you might call a closet writer. At least that's the way it started out. When I wrote my first book I did it in total secrecy. My second book was a private stream of consciousness. By the third book, I was just in the habit of keeping it to myself. Now I have this book—which isn't so much of a book as it is a bound collection of my poems, with some accompanying explanations. This one isn't shrouded in secrecy the way the others were, and the reason is because many have been asking me, for some time now, to compile my poems—gotta give the people what they want—so I've been more open with this one. But first, a little background.

~

How did I become a writer? Well, as Mark Twain once said, one should write about what they know. Since I know my life and, in that, we all have stories to tell, I just began to write. I suppose it's possible I may have had a predisposition for writing because I've always had a penchant for words—they fascinate me. Here's a little piece I wrote back in early 2009 about the wonder of words:

Lusting for Lexicons

What is it about books? How is it that some seem to grip us so? Why are there those that transcend time and remain pertinent throughout the ages? Is there one common denominator found within the literary classics? Think about it—from Homer to Shakespeare, Margaret Mitchell to Louisa May Alcott, even Jane Austen to, dare I say,

M. Hill—what is it about the way a story is constructed that makes it last?

Well, I think the answer is fundamentally simple. It's in the words. Yup, the words. Words are magical; and the way they're strung together on the page, if done right, can almost be like dancing—one continual fluid movement that takes you from one place to another. Step by step, word by word, we vicariously experience different worlds, times and places with the turning of each page. This is why those that resonate with us, emotionally, are always our favorite books. We feel connected—and it's the words that are the connecting sinew.

I love words—they are an unending source of wonder for me: homonyms, synonyms, antonyms. Nouns, verbs, gerunds. Adjectives, adverbs, participles—dangling or otherwise. What kind of a world would we live in without words? Pretty quiet, for one thing—but the question was rhetorical.

I'm not the only one who marvels at words. Take a look at what some others have said regarding these versatile intellectual stimuli:

"Words are, of course, the most powerful drug used by man." ~ Rudyard Kipling

*"To speak **mere words** is much like speaking of **mere dynamite**."* ~ C.J. Ducasse

"The difference between the right word and the almost right word is the difference between lightning and the lightning bug." ~ Mark Twain

I'd be remiss if I didn't include the partial lyric, "Words to memorize, words hypnotize, words make my mouth exercise..." Hey, what ever happened to PWEI? Or was that Violent Femmes?

Anyway, I recently had the opportunity to sit in on a writer's group where one of the exercises was prompted by loose dictionary pages—I got an H page. We were supposed to write something inspired by one of the words, but as I looked at my page, my eyes found focus on a picture of a hawk. Here's what I wrote:

I love the dictionary. Not only is it chock full of information, but it is an endless source of amusement, as well. Yes, that's right, amusement. Looking at page 119 of some disemboweled dictionary, it's the picture of a hawk that catches my eye. A hawk, as almost anyone knows, is any of several predatory birds with blah-blah-blah, yeah, we all know what hawks are. The thing about this hawk is that it recalled a memory of mine from many years ago.

One time I came across the word grebe, and coming from a more urban than rural background, I was not familiar with this word so, naturally, I went to consult The Book. A grebe, as it turns out, is a very small dabchick. Hmph? A dabchick—how 'bout that? See, the thing is, I had no idea what a dabchick was—the dictionary is like that, one word often leads to another; honestly, you could spend days within the pages of a dictionary. I went

*straight to the Ds—d, d, d, dab, dabchick—
there it was. A dabchick is a noun; it is one of
any variety of small grebes.*

*So there you have it—the dictionary—a
funny, funny book!*

It's probably no wonder, with my affinity
for words, that one of my favorite books is, in
fact, the dictionary—that massive collection
of words, those teeny-tiny building blocks,
just waiting to be assembled in such a way as
to tell the next story, to transport you to the
next place, to reveal to you completely new
worlds and experiences... don't even try telling me that's not magical. Forever mystified.

⌒

Okay, so you get it, right? I'm a word nerd. As if
that's not enough, my nephew Michael often calls me
the grammar hammer. What can I say? To quote a very
famous bicep-bulging sailor, I am what I am.

⌒

How did it all begin? Well, innocently enough, like most things.

Many years ago, after first moving to Arizona, I was driving home from church with random thoughts flitting through my brain. As I drove up Dynamite Blvd, my concentration settled on a little box I had stored in my garage. The box was marked "school stuff" and it contained, you guessed it, things from my school days. I transported this box from New Jersey to its new location where it will sit until I die. After moving my life 2,400 miles across our great nation, I declared I would die before I ever moved again. A little dramatic, I know—embracing redundancy, I am what I am. Anyway, I did leaf through the box before shelving it in its eternal resting place. One of the things saved for posterity was a paper I wrote in the fifth grade.

It told the story of Rita. She was considerably older than I was at the time I wrote it but, probably much younger than I was when I rediscovered it. She was a single girl who lived alone with the exception of her cat. In the story, she comes home from work, changes into comfortable clothes, puts on some soft jazz, pours a glass of wine (I know, pretty cutting edge for a 10-year old) and sits down in her cozy apartment with the dark wood and enjoys a good book while her cat curls up on her lap. It may have been raining outside. That's basically it—not so much of a story, more a day-in-the-life type of thing.

It was this little story that captured my attention as I made my way home, and it hit me. I was Rita. Rita with two cats. What a cliché. Single 40-year-old woman with two cats. If I had twenty cats, I'd be eccentric. I'd be the cat lady of Troon North. But I didn't have twenty cats. I had two, which just made me a single 40-year-old woman with two cats. Whoopee-do! As I thought about the comparison, I matter-of-factly stated out loud, "My name is not Rita." Immediately thereafter, I thought that would be a great opening sentence if I were to write a story about my life. And like dominoes, the whole story fell out before me— from opening sentence to closing—*The Ones That Got Away ~ A Dating Memoir* was born. I began writing the moment I got home.

The Ones That Got Away covers forty years of my life so it's on the lengthy side. It's packed with details, which one reviewer questioned the necessity of, but later admitted were necessary seeing as they often substantiated other parts of the story. I didn't hold back—even though I wasn't always shown in the best light—because truth matters. Also, I always felt I was the conservative one of my group and, as such, I didn't think any of the accounts were really all that racy. Well, as my mother used to say—and her mother before her—it wasn't the first time I was wrong and it wouldn't be the last.

I was brimming with enthusiasm over the release of my first book—very proud of it—and perhaps that enthusiasm clouded my judgement as I shared the exciting news with family and friends—both old friends and new. Family, thrilled for me. Old friends, also thrilled. The new friends—those I met at my new church—as you may imagine, some of them didn't fully appreciate my candor, not to mention much of my "history" in general. Hey, a single 40-year-old woman writes a dating memoir—what kind of content would you expect? I don't know why it didn't occur to me that my stories may not have been their cup of tea. As a church-going believer, I know that Jesus didn't come to save the righteous. He came to seek and save the lost. We're all a bunch of non-perfect sinners. He also taught us not to judge, by the way; but, in retrospect, that group probably wasn't the best audience for a book that one reviewer lauded as *"Bridget Jones's Diary* meets *Sex and the City."* Seriously though, are some people that sheltered? Don't they watch TV? Throughout my life I find I'm often surprised by what ruffles people's feathers. Things just don't affect me the same way—maybe because I'm from the Northeast. Back there, everyone sort of just goes with the flow. Collectively, if we had a slogan it would be *whatever*— or *what-evah* for those from Brooklyn.

So even though many enjoyed my book, and I generally have a *whatever* attitude, I did begin to withdraw where it was concerned. Not wanting to be treated like Hester Prynne, I became a little tight-lipped about my past, and my authorship remained a secret for a long time.

~

In spite of my newfound timidity, I was encouraged by some to write a second book. But what would I write about? I already shared my forty-year history; what could possibly have been left unsaid? Not much—although, believe it or not, there were some things that didn't make the final cut. Anyway, I appeased these few fans by telling them that when I was older and put into a home, I would write a sequel called *The Back Forty ~ Waltzing With Widowers*.

With eighty being a long way off, the sequel would just have to wait. I put down my pen, so to speak, and busied myself living my life. Now even though the twilight time of my life may have been a long way off, the distance wasn't as great for my parents. I'd been blessed to have my parents live long and healthy lives, but no one is going to live forever and soon I was faced with that impending reality.

I was a pretty avid hiker at this point in my life and routinely I hiked with my pal Howard. Our conversations were always diverse—from his favorite Woody Allen movies to my time in community theater, from Bertrand Russell (his favorite philosopher) to Bible lessons I was teaching, from deep existential things, like the meaning of life, to inconsequential things like black-eyed peas—the vegetable, not the musical group. The topic grew heavier as my natural father's health slipped into decline.

After my father retired he wasn't very active. This was something that concerned me prior to his retirement. He was the type of man who worked hard providing for his family and did what was necessary, in terms of home maintenance, on his days off. My fear was he didn't have enough interests to maintain a fulfilling life. As his health began to deteriorate, I often shared my thoughts with Howard: What is happening to him? Where is this headed? How many times was I going to grieve this man? Howard wondered what I meant by "times," so I shared with him how I had a heavy heart where my father was concerned throughout much of my life. "This is what you should write about for your next book," he said. As I contemplated his suggestion, I halfheartedly replied, "Well, it wouldn't be a funny book, that's for sure."

I decided the act of getting my feelings down on paper would be, at the very least, cathartic for me, so I began to write what would become *Unconditional ~ A Story of Love and Loss*.

I began the story a couple of years before my father passed, and in that time I nearly lost my stepfather, ultimately did lose my father and subsequently lost my mother. My second book turned out to be an intimate look at my heart turned inside out in a deep exploration of unconditional love.

The topic was so extremely personal—I put things on paper that I hadn't ever shared with anyone before—so apart from Howard, no one knew of this book's existence. Even Howard had no idea that I had been working at it on and off over the years, let alone completed it. So it remained a secret until I decided to share it with my stepfather, who was so moved by it, he insisted I make it available for distribution. He thought it was absolutely beautiful and he told me it helped him with his own grief. No higher praise.

~

So, I was the author of two books. Who knew? Most people don't write even one. I think it was Aristotle who claimed one's life would not be complete if not for accomplishing three things: 1. Build a house. Did it. 2. Raise a child. I've taught hundreds of 'em in Sunday school so that ought to count, not to mention my involvement with the offspring of my siblings. 3. Write a book. Done! (Twice.)

Seriously, though, write a book? How about that? I get it, though. See, the thing is, all of us have a story to tell—it may not always be the most interesting story, but it's ours and if we can tell it in an entertaining fashion, then why not? You never know who is going to enjoy it, relate to it, learn, grow and benefit from it.

I now had two books under my belt and no intention of writing a third. After all, what would I write about? My first book was inspired by a fleeting memory and the second from what was initially an emotional-cleansing exercise. But then it happened. I got the phone call that was the impetus for book number three.

We were just back from Alaska when my dad (stepfather) called to tell me that his bridge came out—and, apparently, it was my fault because I was the one who mistakenly bought the incorrect candy for our vacation snack bag. This was the phone call I received and it's an abridged version to the beginning of *The Butterscotch Chronicles ~ An Anecdotal Look at Aging*.

After dealing with the dental situation, I began to ponder the whole butterscotch phenomenon. I don't think that's too strong a word; in fact, I think it is the correct word, exactly. A phenomenon is defined as *a fact or situation that is observed to exist or happen, especially one whose cause or explanation is in question.* Typically, it is not uncommon to find those from within the older population to have butterscotch candies on hand, and here's the question: *When* does this happen? Is this a habit resulting from a conscious decision or do the candies just mysteriously appear one day after one reaches a certain age? Lost in the contemplation of it all, I wondered how old I might be when I find these tasty treats in the bottom of my purse.

With that, I began to think of the many changes I already endured throughout the entire aging process to date. And, although I may be keen on a little secrecy every now and then, I wondered why most of what happens to our bodies isn't openly discussed, why all the secrecy there? Most of us share similar experiences. Is it just in poor taste to discuss these things? Does it go against social decorum? Would it ruffle the feathers of the etiquette police? Well, you know what I say... *whatever!* Not one to break tradition, I kept the anecdotal account of my aging body traveling down the road of life under wraps until it was complete and released for distribution.

After the release of *Butterscotch* I found myself, once again, being asked about my next book. I told the inquirers that I didn't have any plans for another book—I needed to be inspired, I offered up by way of further explanation. More than a few of them said I should do something with my poems. You may have been wondering when I was going to address the poetry aspect of this book. Well, here it is.

When I was much younger I used to write poems (using the word loosely). One of my childhood friends reminded me how I wrote poems about my natural father when I was in middle school. I didn't even remember that. I do remember writing silly little poems when I was college-age, either about a particular person or event. There were even times, at parties, when I'd be asked by veritable strangers to write a poem for them. I'd ask them to tell me things about their lives that they'd like to see in the poem, then spend a few minutes constructing it. I had a knack for formulating details in rhyme about something specific.

Now a poet is a person possessing special powers of imagination or expression, who writes poems. So, although I meet the technical definition, I certainly do not consider myself a classical poet. Think about Robert Frost, "Two roads diverged in a wood, and I took the one less traveled..." Introspective. Or Dylan Thomas, "Do not go gentle into that goodnight... rage, rage against the dying of the light." Deep. Or my favorite, Joyce Kilmer, "Poems are made by fools like me, but only God can make a tree." Profound. No, my poems can't compare to these. But they are fun for me. Something will strike me and I'll have a flash of inspiration. When this happens I immediately jot down ideas so as not to lose the intensity or charge of the intention. Then I assemble, tweak and finesse the words into a playful composition.

I'm primarily Irish and German. And I accredit my Irish heritage with my ability to tell stories in an entertaining fashion. As far as rhyme goes, my natural father also wrote poetry, so my skill could be an apple-falling-not-far-from-the-tree type of thing. I never saw any of his poetry. I know he wrote for my mother, and he wrote for my stepmother as well. I suspect his poetry was along the lines of the romantic poets, like Keats, but I don't know for sure. Even without seeing any of his works, though, I'm pretty sure his style wasn't like mine. Mine is a cross between, say, traditional iambic pentameter and… Dr. Seuss—with a splash of Clement Moore. So I'm not deep, generally speaking—but I do have few poems with a little bit of depth to them.

There's a line in Peter Gabriel's song *Mercy Street*—about poet Anne Sexton—that I relate to, which says "words support like bone." She was deeply troubled. I am not; but, when I do occasionally find myself mired in the rut of monotony, I often turn to my writing for a little saving grace. So…

Without further delay
Let's get underway,
And take a swift look
At the poems in this book.

Just a quick reminder,
Here at the start—
Inspired by life,
These poems come from my heart.

Some are short, some are long;
Some are silly, some sweet.

With quite a variety,
May each one be a treat.

Some may be shallow,
Some may be deep,
Some might make you laugh,
For some, you might weep.

There are those that are quirky;
And those that are tender,
Those you'll connect with
And those you'll remember.

Overall they are light and meant to delight;
So sit for a while—my wish is you'll smile.
This is it, we've arrived, at the jumping-off place.
And here they are now for your welcome embrace.

Creepy-Crawlies 〜

October is the perfect month for Halloween—the days are shorter, the air is crisp and there's a slight howling to the sound of the nighttime wind. Leaves blow around and trees look dead. Throw a full moon in there and you have all the makings for a full-on creep fest.

Halloween, as it's become, is a far cry from its Festival of the Dead origins. I don't believe that spirits rise and wreak havoc on this day, as some do; no, for me, I think of Halloween as a day for kids to dress up in costumes and amass a lot of candy. Still, with that said—and even though it's just one day—I think all the associated autumn decorations can add a certain degree of spookiness to the entire month of October. A spookiness that could make someone a little jumpy, maybe... especially if that someone is me—someone who gets creeped out by little things like those fake spider rings that kids like to leave lying around. And, if I don't care for fake spiders, you can bet I'm not that fond of the real ones. Now listen, spiders outside— even tarantulas—don't really bother me, but in my house, that's a different story.

My blood ran cold and my heart skipped a beat as my breath caught in my throat one night when I came home late to find a spider the size of a plum clinging to my kitchen wall up where it meets the ceiling. As I stood there, frozen in fear, I couldn't imagine what I was going to do. My ceilings are twelve feet high. I knew I couldn't leave it there. What if it wandered off? Where would it go? Where might it lay eggs? These are just a few of the things that went through my mind as my heartbeat picked up speed and I began to perspire. I mulled over my options: call my brother for help, no; spray with Raid thereby saturating my wall and ceiling, no; *could* I leave it there, no—definitely not. I knew what had to be done and I was the one who was going to have to do it.

I steeled my resolve and got the necessary supplies—namely, a telescoping duster and what I call my scorpion killer, which is really just a Swiffer sweeper wrapped in paper towel. (That's a story for a different day.) The plan was to stand on a stool and, using the fully extended duster, fling the eight-legged wonder to the floor, after which I'd hop down and exterminate this poor in-the-wrong-place-at-the-wrong-time creature with the use of my previously prepared squisher Swiffer.

Here's where my plan went awry. Standing on the stool, I had to stretch over my hutch to reach this thing, and as the duster grazed one or two of its legs, it didn't fling him—as I had hoped—but merely knocked him off his perch. I nearly fell off my own perch as the spider wafted down the wall and fell behind the hutch. I quickly grabbed the Swiffer and got on my knees to locate the fallen threat on the floor beneath the hutch. The problem was he wasn't there. Oh my.

I was in a full-body sweat at this point. Where did it go? Placing my cheek to the wall, I strained to look into the half-inch space *behind* the hutch. Ugh, there he was, clinging to the back of the hutch, hanging on like... like... well, like Spiderman. *Now* what was I going to do? That hutch weighs a ton and it was too close to the wall to get anything behind it. It's amazing what a little adrenaline can do, though. I managed to budge it about an inch and a half, and still, my adversary held fast. This was becoming a battle of wills.

I once again grabbed the extended duster. I swooshed it along the back of the hutch. I missed. I swooshed again. Success! He dropped to the floor. I grabbed the Swiffer and pushed it back and forth under the hutch until the paper towel revealed the telltale wet spot of a spider that once was. Legs loosely strewn about proved I had squished him into oblivion. It was horrible, but I did what I had to do. Many of our spiders are poisonous and I couldn't just leave it there.

As my exterminating-induced anxiety subsided, draining my body of energy, I did what any sane person who had just suffered a mild trauma would do, I wrote a poem.

Creepy-Crawlies

I do not advocate killing.
Be certain, it is not thrilling;
But when the fear is absolutely bone-chilling,
You've just got to be willing.

They'll creep and they'll crawl,
And they'll cling to your wall;
With eight legs in all,
They're not likely to fall.

Some are tan, some are brown, some are black—
All will send chills up your back.
You cannot cut any slack,
You must give them a whack.

You simply can't risk being bitten—
These are lethal spiders, not kittens.
For "kill or be killed," it is written;
So, adios, Spidey—good riddance!

Pumpkin Pitch ～

It was shortly after my move to Arizona when I got involved in my local church. As the congregation was rapidly increasing, they had a growing need for a wide variety of volunteers to help support their efforts.

Greeters are rarely hard to come by—unless you're talking about greeting in the parking lot, that is. Those positions are a little more difficult to fill. Well, they didn't have a shortage of inside greeters and I, like the masses, had no desire to stand outside in the heat and sun waving to folks rushing in on two wheels.

There's always a need in the hospitality arena, but making coffee and cutting up donuts didn't feel like a good fit for me either.

Of course the increase in family attendance naturally meant an increase in children and, therefore, the Kids Ministry was severely understaffed. Many

shy away from children—even those who have some
of their own—but I don't. Even still, I didn't feel
adequate to teach, but I could certainly be a helper,
so this is the area I chose to get involved in. As fate
would have it, it wasn't too long before the adult I was
assisting stepped down. This turn of events found me
placed in the teaching role, and revealed to me a gift I
was unaware I had. Apparently, not only can I relate
to the kiddos, but they respond to me as well and, as
such, Miss Melissa was born. (Ironic, isn't it—as an
adult I'm Missy, but to the children I'm Miss Melissa?)

With my newfound role, it was a no-brainer for
me to assist with the church's biggest community out-
reach event of the year—their Fall Festival. Spread out
all over our campus were carnival games of chance and
craft tents. We also had go-kart riding, laser tag and a
dunk tank, not to mention all the food booths with
hot dogs, popcorn and cotton candy. At every station
we had enormous buckets of candy to satisfy the trick-
or-treat aspect of the season.

Each year I manned the Pumpkin Pitch booth,
which was really designed for toddler-aged kids, but
frequented by many of my students no matter their
ages. I painted a hollowed-out pumpkin to look like

27

Spiderman—always a crowd pleaser—then placed it in an alcove created by lollipop-infested hay bales. The idea was to toss (read: drop directly in) a tiny ball into Spidey the pumpkin. Handfuls of candy granted to all who achieved the easily attainable goal. Fun was routinely had by all.

Here's the poem I wrote for this event:

Pumpkin Pitch

Hay bales, pumpkins, costumes and more—
Carnival games and candy galore;
With tricks, treats and everything sweet,
Highlands' Fall Festival cannot be beat!

Thousands of people will come, that's for sure;
But it's really the kids who we do it all for.
They'll be there in droves—in masquerade clothes—
Having the time of their lives, as everyone knows.

Buzz Lightyear will be there, and a Batman or two,
Mr. Incredible and Winnie the Pooh.

Belle and her friends will be there this night—
Cinderella, Jasmine and, of course, Snow White.

Darth Vadars, Tiggers and black cats will abound;
Devils and angels will easily be found.
Spidermen, vampires and hobos in rags
Will play freely together, filling their bags.

There'll be Snickers, Skittles, Kit-Kats and Nerds,
Dum-Dum lollipops and things that go squirt;
Starburst, Tootsies, worms and bears—oh so gummy,
And hundreds of other things good for the tummy.

Chocolates, caramels and gum drops, too—
Peppermint Patties and a Charleston Chew;
M&Ms, Reese's and the famed Baby Ruth,
Will satisfy each and every sweet tooth.

After a few frenzied hours, it will come to an end;
But we'll set it up next year and do it again!

TRADITIONS ～

The church's Fall Festival became a tradition for me. I had a sixth-grade teacher who once asked our class why we keep traditions. At eleven years of age, a lot of us didn't initially understand what she meant. Mrs. Dickerson was talking about holidays, rituals and customs, of course. Why do we have them? The answer is too deep for a child to really understand. We have them because they anchor us to who we are, our past, and what's important to us.

Fall kicks off a busy tradition-filled season what with festivals, Thanksgiving and especially Christmas—the mother of all tradition-filled holidays. It's not surprising to think about Christmas when we're talking about holiday traditions. For most of us, there's a routine we typically follow each time the yuletide season rolls around: cards are written, we make (and eat) lots of tasty treats, homes get decorated. We write our lists—and check them twice—ensuring we don't miss a single thing.

I mail out Christmas cards right after Thanksgiving. In many of the cards I receive, "Yours was the first one I got this year," is written in as a P.S. For these folks, that kicks off their holidays—"Oh, her card is here, 'tis the season!"

I make peanut brittle each year for a few people who tell me Christmas wouldn't be Christmas without it—and, naturally, that's why I do it. Also, following the tradition of my grandmother, I send holiday petit fours from The Swiss Colony to my closest friends.

And, of course, the biggie—I decorate my house the very same day I put away the autumn decorations. No better example for the passing of time than to box up what's past and prep for what's coming.

It used to be when my family came over, my nephew was the one who'd marvel at all the decorations. "I turned the lights on in the village," he'd say with glee. "They were waiting for you," I'd gently reply. Already knowing the answer, he'd lightheartedly ask, "Are there Nestlé Crunch jingle bells in the snowman jar?" Amused, I'd just respond with a simple, "Yes." After all, that's why they were there—I knew he was going to ask. "Oh, I love this guy," he'd say as he tumbled the small Santa shaker ball that enthralled him for years. Taking it all in, I'd smile and say, "I know you do."

His joy became part of my tradition and even though he's older now—no longer lighting the village, auditing the Nestlé Crunch jingle bell supply, or shaking the little Santa snow globe—I'll remember his childhood enthusiasm and cherish the memories attached to those things. Traditions are the ties that bind.

When speaking of Christmas and traditions, I'd be remiss if I didn't address my specific holiday tradition with Danny Aiello. Yes, Danny Aiello—the actor.

Before the retail industry went wild, it used to be Thanksgiving that launched the holiday season. Generally, the festivities were kicked off with the aforementioned, unusually large, autumn-themed dinner—I mean, does anyone actually make parsnips at any other time of the year? But I digress. Then, before the bloating even subsided, there were those setting their alarm clocks for the early a.m.—so early, that for some, it was still considered night—just to dash off to the early-early-early-bird Black Friday special sales that insanely vie for all the overeager shoppers.

When I first moved to Arizona, my sister-in-law used to invite me along for the big Black Friday shopping bonanza, but each year, after thanking her for including me, I'd decline. It wasn't just because I'm not that much of a shopper—although I'm not; and it wasn't that twelve hours in a mall would probably kill me—although it probably would; and, it had little to do with the fact that by Black Friday nearly all my holiday shopping was done—although it always is; it was just that I had my own way of spending the day after Thanksgiving.

I traditionally use this bonus day to put out all my Christmas decorations and ready the house for the season. I have a wide variety of holiday decorations, knickknacks and tchotchkes that I've amassed over the years. There is hardly an available square inch of space in my home that doesn't have a Christmas something, sitting there, beckoning good cheer. Honestly, if I put price tags on everything that's displayed, my home would look like a gift shop! Anyway, I am inordinately organized (with just a splash of OCD) so it's probably needless to say but, I have a system. After the autumn decorations are repacked and stowed in the garage, I stash away all my regular stuff, after which I dust the furniture, then bring in the boxes.

These boxes aren't just filled with tangible items—no, they're filled with memories, too. Memories of decorating my first apartment, memories of chilly holiday shopping in historic Smithville, and through the nostalgia inspired by my Kinkade (Thomas, not Reuben) Christmas village, many memories of Christmases past. The thing is, with all these memories that I routinely unpack, there is one that I never seem to remember until I actually see it again.

I have a very large decorative bowl that I fill each year with red glass ornaments—they're not expensive, in fact, each box was less than five dollars, but they are fragile, and so, to protect them while they're stored away, I have them wrapped in a few sheets of newspaper—a sleeve for each box. Filling this bowl is one of the first things I do as I begin to adorn the house—and *that* is when I'm reminded of Danny Aiello. You may have been wondering when and how Danny was going to enter the picture. See, there is a feature story about him, accompanied by a large photo, on one of the papers that covers the glass balls. As I remove the ornaments from the sleeve, I usually smile and say to myself, "Ah, another Christmas with Danny Aiello." Assuming the date on the paper is accurate, and there's no reason to think otherwise, he has been with me since 1993. At this point, Christmas wouldn't be the same without him.

Between Mrs. Dickerson and Mr. Aiello how could I not write a poem about traditions?

Traditions

We all have our traditions
That keep the holidays hopping—
From turkey on Thanksgiving
To Black Friday shopping.

We have holiday lights
And decorations that charm,
And family trips
To the local tree farm.

We have Christmas wrappings
With ribbons and bows,

Tinsel and garland
And Rudolph's nose.

We send greeting cards
To friends far and near;
And sing Christmas carols—
The ones we hold dear.

There's peppermint sticks,
And old St. Nick,
Cookies and eggnog
That's creamy and thick.

There's Charlie Brown, Ralphie,
And the Baileys, too;
But Christmas wouldn't be Christmas,
Without you know who.

Baby Jesus was born,
So tiny and small—
For you and for me,
For one and for all.

That's why we celebrate
Christmas each year.
That's why we're filled
With holiday cheer.

So hang up the mistletoe
And roll out the holly,
Christmas is coming—
It's time to be jolly.

I bid you Merry Christmas
And a Ho! Ho! Ho!
But not just from me—
From me and Danny Aiello!

Happy New Year ～

As you can see, the holidays inspire me. Rounding out the fourth quarter festivities is New Year's—Eve and Day, I suppose. Now I don't know about you, but New Year's never feels like the first holiday of the year—it always feels like the last, right? It caps off the crisp Christmas season.

When I first moved out to Arizona there were more than a few who wondered if I'd miss the change of seasons. Truth be told, we all hear this kind of thing a lot. "Oh, I could never live there—I'd miss the change of seasons." Well, we may not have deciduous trees with colorful fall foliage, but we do get a change in seasons—we get two: Christmas and summer. But, I kid! Seriously, though, we do get chilly weather in the winter months, which always enhances the holidays, but once Christmas is past, I am more than ready for some warmer weather and it is not uncommon to find me lamenting, "When will this winter ever end?"

The following poem was penned for the kickoff of 2009:

Happy New Year

Christmas is over.
The New Year's begun.
I've had it with winter;
I'm ready for sun.

I'm spoiled rotten—
I know it, it's true;
But I've lived here five years now,
So what can I do?

Temps in the 40s!
I can't take it that chilly.
I'm from the Northeast
So I know that sounds silly.

I don't mean to cry,
Whine, mope or sulk;
But who can move
Wrapped up in this bulk?

The turtlenecks, fleeces
And warm woolen sweaters
Get the job done
But what would be better...

Is if temperatures rose
Just up a bit, see—
60 or 70
Is quite nice to me.

But, alas, I must wait
A little while longer,
For our hot desert sun
To grow a bit stronger.

Just a few more weeks now—
Not as long as you'd think.
In fact, summer will be here
Before I can blink.

Why do I rush things
The way that I do?
Because I haven't got patience—
It's an elusive virtue.

That's what I'll work on—
Yes, that should be fine.
What a good resolution
For 2009.

With the future before us,
Wide open and clear,
Let's embrace it fully—
Have a Happy New Year!

Achoo ～

Not a lot of people are comfortable with the word muculent. I like it, though. I've liked it from the moment I first heard it, which was way back when I was in high school. Something about it just stuck with me—no pun intended. If you're new to this word, the pun clarification will be lost on you.

There are a lot of words out there which, unless you're already familiar with them, don't offer any clue as to what they actually mean. Well, this isn't one of them. This is one of those words that you can ascertain its definition just by the initial pronunciation of it. *Muke*...does anything else come to mind other than mucus? Nope, not for me, and I'm betting not for you, either. Simultaneously, as the thought of mucus comes to mind, the natural inclination is to slightly repress your gag reflex. And that's the other cool thing about this word. Not only can you guess what it means, but it actually evokes the appropriate visceral response, too. It's powerful.

So, other than being icky, what is mucus, technically speaking? According to Medicinenet.com "Mucus is a normal, slippery and stringy fluid substance produced by many lining tissues in the body. It is essential for body function and acts as a protective and moisturizing layer to keep critical organs from drying out. Mucus also acts as a trap for irritants like dust, smoke, or bacteria. It contains antibodies and bacteria-killing enzymes to help fight off infections." Okay, so, in spite of its grossness, it's pretty important stuff—essential was the word they used. I don't dispute the importance of it, but what happens when it begins to run amok?

When mucus is mass produced in my sinuses, it very often drains down the back of my throat (who's repressing gag reflexes now?) in the form of post-nasal drip, where as it clings to my vocal cords, it almost always has an adverse reaction rendering me speechless with laryngitis. This has plagued me throughout my whole life—my Achilles heel, if you will. It was during one of these episodes that I penned the following:

Achoo

I cannot seem to concentrate.
Everything's a chore, of late.
My head is pounding
And I can't think straight.

Itchy, runny eyes that tear—
Discomfort fills my inner ear;
Inflammation grows
And I can barely hear.

My eyes flutter and almost close
As pressure in my sinus grows;
Tingling sensations
Tickle my nose.

I'm sneezing, wheezing
And barely breathing;
My lips are chapped raw
From chronic mouth-breathing.

Pain in my throat makes me weak.
Mercy and comfort are what I seek.

I can no longer swallow,
Nor can I speak.

Yes, laryngitis—that's my thing,
With a choking phlegm that really clings.
I pray for the relief
A healing would bring.

It's everyday stress
And mental duress
That's making me
Such a physical mess.

I gargle and sleep—
And try not to weep;
I don't complain much
Since I can't make a peep.

The dry cough I could do without—
Hacking like that just wears me out;
But that's what's next,
I have no doubt.

Time after time,
It's the same, I find.
So I know I'll fight
This mucus and slime.

Getting better, I cannot force—
This just has to run its course;
And when my voice returns,
It will be hoarse.

But that's okay, I say to myself...
Thinking about what is true wealth;
It's certainly not riches,
It's more about health.

So, this will pass and go away,
I'm looking forward to that day—
But until it gets here,
What can I say?

Winter colds blow!

RESURRECTION SUNDAY ∼

Since I grew up in the Christian faith, the Sunday following Good Friday was always known as Easter Sunday. After years of bouncing around a few of the denominational Christian faiths, somewhere in my early forties, after attending a non-denominational Bible-teaching church, I became born-again. For those not familiar with this term, it simply means that one has had a spiritual rebirth—hence, born-again. So now, as a born-again, Bible-studying believer, I tend to think of the Sunday following Good Friday as Resurrection Sunday.

To me, this is the highest, most holy of all the holidays. More important than Christmas. Although, I do recognize that Jesus first had to be born in order to fulfill all the subsequent events. That's why his birth is so wondrous. It sets in motion the beginning of the end of the whole plan. But, it truly is the end of the whole plan—the resurrection—that changed the world.

I'm not going to get into a theological dissertation on the resurrection, that's not what this is about—you can do your own research—there's plenty of proof and evidence for this blessed event. What this is about is bunnies and jelly beans.

Prior to being born-again, I never really questioned any aspect of the Easter bunny tradition; but somewhere along the line, it began to make less sense to me. What makes even less sense are those who are not believers, who "celebrate" Easter anyway, with the goody-filled pastel-colored Easter baskets and family dinners. I asked one such individual, "What exactly are you celebrating?" His explanation was weak, at best, as he fumbled through his rationale of spreading joy by giving his kids chocolate bunnies. I remained perplexed. I mean, why not celebrate... could be anything... how about, say, aviation? You can hand out little plane-shaped Sweet-Tarts in teeny-tiny airport hangars—that would make about as much sense.

Don't misunderstand me here. I am not some religious zealot without a sense of humor. In fact, to this day, one of my favorite cartoon drawings is of an Easter theme. In it, there are two chocolate Easter bunnies facing each other. One has teeth marks where his tail used to be and the other has had his ears broken off. The one says, "My butt hurts." And the other responds, "What?" I think this is clever and it never fails to make me chuckle.

Easter occurs each spring. Spring is the season of rebirth—prolific bunnies frolicking all over the place (especially out here in the desert), new foliage emerging and blooming, baby birds happily singing as they welcome each new day. There are many elements of spring that coincide with the Easter holiday, but when you compare the two, the contrast is stark.

Resurrection Sunday

Riding into town like a king...
Oh, the joy that comes with spring.

Silently enduring bogus trials...
Oh, to see the kiddos' smiles.

A nail for each hand and one for his feet...
The fun of an egg hunt cannot be beat.

"Forgive them," he asks, "they know not what they do."
Who is he talking about—them, me or you?

"It is finished," he cried, just before dying...
Oh, the thrill of Easter egg dyeing.

His body was placed in a tomb, not a casket...
Grab hold of those bunnies and fill up that basket!

Prophecies fulfilled, three days later he rose...
Oh, the parades, fancy bonnets and bows.

Why do we celebrate Easter this way—
Nesting sugary treats on fake beds of hay?

It's the resurrection of Jesus, have no doubt,
That's what Easter is truly about.

RAIN, RAIN, GO AWAY ～

I am a Jersey girl—born and raised, as they say—who grew up in one of the coastal counties of the Garden State. I lived there for 39 years before I packed up and moved my life west to Arizona. Prior to my move, a lot of folks asked me if I was concerned, at all, about the heat. I told them, "No, not *at all*." The reason I had no concern was because, until I hit menopause, I was one of those people who are always chilly. You know the type, wearing a sweatshirt at the shore because of the cool night air. Annoying to some—I don't know why.

Anyway, I didn't move across the country for the weather, that's always just been a bonus. There are many parts of this state that experience a wide variety of weather conditions, but the Phoenix Metro Valley isn't one of them. On average, we have over 300 pleasant days of sunshine—which leaves only a few days that may be considered unpleasant. This is what's truly appealing about living here—weather rarely impacts any plans you may have.

Long before seasonal affective disorder—or S.A.D., appropriately enough—was a commonly discussed condition, I could have told you it existed. In New Jersey, they claim there are about 200 days of sunshine. I think they're being overly generous with that stat; but even if they're not, that leaves 165 days of inclement weather. I remember one year in particular when it rained EVERY weekend between Memorial Day and Labor Day. As you can imagine, this was devastating to the Jersey shore economy. Not to mention a major bummer for all the working stiffs who habitually remained at their desks while the sun shone gloriously throughout each week. And it may have been this same year, too, when the extremely wet summer not only caused constant flooding, but created an overabundant growth of mossy green mold—it could be found flourishing on tree trunks, in the corners of concrete patios or coating wooden decks—it was everywhere. Ugh! The rainy days, as the song goes, always get me down. Seriously, the pall of living under the low ceiling of murky precipitous clouds is enough to dampen anybody's mood. In an effort to combat the bleak, atmospheric psychological impact, I'd often try to imagine the sun shining brilliantly just above the low-lying layer of gloom. Or, if I was watching any TV show where it was sunny out, I'd try and mentally immerse myself into the scenery. So, you can clearly see, for me, the desert offers a lot of appeal.

I settled in the northeast part of the valley, in Scottsdale, where our annual rainfall is roughly seven inches—just a tiny bit over half a foot. In comparison, Jackson, NJ, gets about 49 inches of rain in a year—just a tiny bit over four feet! With such a comparatively reduced amount of rain, one might think when it does actually precipitate here, it would be regarded as a special event—and it is, for a lot of the folks, but I am not one of them. When it rains here, my sister-in-law likes to sit outside on her patio and watch it. When my niece and nephew were small, they liked to stand outside in it—much like I did as a kid during the first snowfall. And my dad keeps track of it, announcing how many days it's been since the last rainfall. He'll inform me that it's been such and such number of days since we've had rain, and I'm always a little surprised. I'll reply, "Really—that many, huh?"

while silently thinking I could still do without it. Now, I am not an idiot, and I know it's a fundamental, basic necessity to life. I just wish it would be a fundamental, basic necessity *overnight*.

Well, with your newfound understanding for my lack of affinity for the life-giving sprinkles from the sky, it should be no surprise to you to hear that I was very unhappy during a particular February when we received our annual rainfall in one month—and the shortest month, at that. Naturally, I found inspiration in the bizarre meteorological conditions of early 2010.

Rain, Rain, Go Away

They say El Niño is the reason
We've had so much rain this season.
Seven inches is the aggregate sum—
Over 12 months, though, not just one!

I don't mean to be cranky; I don't want to complain.
But I can't take one more day of rain.
I try not to be grumpy or get upset,
But it's the desert—and it shouldn't be wet!

Everything's soggy—puddles abound;
Our poor saguaros are falling down.
Those good ol' boys—so old, so tall—
Can't take this much rain, at all.

Rain is essential for life, I know.
It is our friend and not our foe.
I understand this and know that it's true,
But I'm a little spoiled, what can I do?

Typically our days are sunny.
And all this rain isn't funny.
I'd like blue skies back, that's for sure—
Because as I said, I can't take much more.

But, oh, the beauty this rain will bring;
We're sure to have an awesome spring.
We'll see the bright side to all these showers,
When the desert's awash with wildflowers.

It won't be too long until our days
Are filled once again with beaming rays;
Then we'll get back to outdoor fun,
Living life in the Valley of the Sun.

Period! ~

When you take a look at all the species, particularly mammals, I don't think you'll find any who enjoy a good party more than humans do. Granted, we are the only ones who spend the majority of our waking hours at work; other groups primarily spend their time in social settings—just eating, sleeping and generally living—so they don't need the break from toil the way we do.

We not only enjoy the respite from work, but we actually need it for our overall health and well-being and, as such, we rarely miss an opportunity for celebration. As previously mentioned, we celebrate some sacred holidays like Christmas and Easter with rooted traditions. Others offer up lots of fun and food, like Halloween and Thanksgiving. Some special days don't warrant the big family gatherings, but recognizing historical people of influence is always a celebratory cause for selling mattresses and appliances at low discount prices—think MLK Day, President's Day and, yes, even Columbus Day (for those who eschew political correctness)—plus, for many bankers and federal employees, it's another day of paid time off. Hooray!

We relish the holidays that bookend the summer—a full party season in its own right. Memorial Day should have never morphed into backyard block parties, but who doesn't enjoy a nice outdoor barbecue? Labor Day marks the last hurrah of summer—a sobering dose of reality eased with hearty platefuls of hot dogs, hamburgers and side salads galore. And we have wild New Year's Eve bashes along with reflective New Year's Day dinners to bookend complete years.

Never missing a chance to celebrate, we like to recognize a couple of saints—Valentine and Patrick, to be specific—which, let's be honest, is really just an excuse to guiltlessly eat luscious chocolate and blithely drink green beer.

We esteem our flag on the Fourteenth of June and light up the sky with fireworks on the Fourth of July as we commemorate our nation's birth. Being internationally broad-minded, we like to partake in the revelry of Cinco de Mayo, which has nothing to do with Mexican independence but rather a celebration of their victory over France in what is known as the Battle of Puebla. And here again the French lose. They have missed the boat in promoting their own battle victory when they stormed the Bastille—a crucial turning point in the French Revolution. Think about it, we could be participating in Fête du Fromage festivals on July 14 with an array of tasty cheese tartlets, varieties of mac-n-cheese, artisan cheeses paired with appropriate wines and mini croques—both Monsieur et Madame. Give us any reason to sabotage a sensible diet and we are happy to comply.

As a society, we enjoy celebration. We honor the special roles people have: Mother's Day, Father's Day and Grandparents Day. We even have a day just for fools! And let's not be remiss, each of us have our own birthdays to share with loved ones over cake and ice cream.

There is quite a lucrative industry surrounding all these special days. Most pharmacies and supermarkets have more than a few aisles specifically dedicated to greeting cards. There are birthday cards for grandfathers, fathers, husbands, brothers, uncles, nephews and sons—the blue section. In the pink section you find cards for nannies, mothers, wives, sisters, aunts, nieces and daughters. Mixed in, of course, are all the step, half and adoptive versions of these relations. Plus, there are all the other cards. There's a wide variety of congratulatory cards—for your new home, recent move, job promotion, graduation, as well as blessed events like Communion, Confirmation and Mitzvahs both Bah- and Bat-. There are cards for engagements, weddings and those surrounding new babies—be it birth or baptism. There's an array of sympathy cards offering condolences for the loss of loved ones—people as well as pets. There are thank-you cards, cards of encouragement and those just to say hello. I mean, if you need a card, the folks at companies like American Greetings and Hallmark have got you covered. They offer a vast selection of sentiments for nearly every occasion—and if they've missed any, you're welcome to choose from an assortment of blank cards where you can write your own specific note.

So, we like to party and send supportive notes for milestones and achievements, which is generally a good thing, but somehow I think we've gone a little too far. I wrote about this in *The Butterscotch*

Chronicles, but I'm repeating it here since this book is a compilation of my many poems. Apparently modern mothers everywhere have begun to host "first period" parties. I kid you not. To say I was nonplussed when I first heard about this is not an understatement. I just couldn't imagine what a card would say for this type of event. But then I did.

Period!

Adolescence is over,
It's come to an end.
And now you have,
A new monthly friend.

You've hit puberty,
Let's shout for joy.
Good-bye, little girl—
Oh, boy! Oh, boy!

Expect some cramps,
And bloating, too.

A Collection of Poems

You're shedding a lining,
  It's not easy to do.

Your head may ache
And moods will swing,
But you can procreate—
  That's a cool thing.

So what if it's painful,
And you retain water?
You're a woman now,
My sweet baby daughter.

Congratulations on your first period, Honey!

A COUPLE OF ODES ∿

I always thought of an ode as a type of dedication poem—be it to a skylark or autumn—with something special about it, but technically it's a lyric poem characterized by lofty feelings. I can't say my feelings were ever lofty, but I have dedicated a couple of verses to two specific individuals. The first is a petit larcenist and the second is a cosmic tormentor. Naturally, before the ode, I have an intro for each.

∿

I'm a newspaper subscriber. I know, they say no one's buying papers anymore—I suppose what's really said is that no one is reading papers anymore. And, in spite of the fact that I get regular home delivery, I do sort of fall into that category. I'll admit that I do not get the paper to stay up on events—current or otherwise—although, I do scan the headlines. No, I get the paper for the puzzles. Translation = big dork. There, I've said it. Hey, I'm not the only one who does puzzles, you know. It's people like me who make big business for others. Think about it, where would Will Shortz be without all of us puzzlers?

There are others, too, whose entire careers lie in creating brainteasers for people like me—addicts, who are hooked on solving these mental conundrums. I know I'm digressing but what non-puzzlers don't realize is that these things really do stimulate the brain, and if you do them like I do, over lunch, it helps to pace one's ingestion and, therefore, digestion. If not for the puzzles, I'd inhale my lunch in four minutes flat. But, as I said, I've digressed.

So, I've been getting home delivery since I moved here. Every morning, no matter what time I'm up (as early as 4:30 a.m. in the summer) my paper is always there, in my driveway, waiting for me. I have a very dependable carrier. I've never met him, but we exchange Christmas cards every year. Without fail, sometime during the middle of December, folded within the newsprint, I find a greeting card wishing me all the

best for the holiday season. This enables me to recip-
rocate with yuletide wishes of my own along with a
gesture of appreciation for his steadfast commitment.

I assume my carrier is an elderly gentleman—
possibly a retired veteran. I say elderly because his
name is Newton. You just don't see that name much
anymore—at least not among the younger generation,
that's for sure. And I say retired vet because of his re-
liability and dedication to his customers. I've already
told you how my paper is always there, but it's also
always tucked safely away in a plastic protective sleeve,
and on the rare days we have rain, he double bags the
paper. This is no slouch, this is someone who takes
pride in his work.

Now this is where I have an issue. (You knew
I had to have one.) Lately, someone—a likely dog
walker, indeed—is taking the plastic bags off my paper (read: stealing). I'm sure the perpetrator (correct
word for an alleged crime committer) doesn't think
there's anything wrong with this. In fact, I'd bet they
just assume I discard the bags once I bring the paper
inside. And guess what? They're right. But that's not
really the point, is it?

Newton places my paper in the protective—

operative word here—bag for a reason: To protect it. Newsprint is already filthy. Do I need road dust and grime all over my paper, too? Or how about bird poop? That's always nice to see while the paper sits on my kitchen island—where I eat! One day it drizzled and my paper was dotted with water marks. And another time, on a breezy day, I had to retrieve wind strewn papers from my front yard. Should I have to tolerate this? No, I don't think so. It's my paper—I'm paying for it—and it's my sleeve. It should remain on the paper, protecting it, until such time when *I* remove it.

As I said, I don't think the thief sees the crime, and I certainly don't mean to be petty, but it is my property. I mean, how cheap can you be? If you're a dog walker and you know you need to pick up poop, buy a box of bags already.

Well, I did just that. I bought a box of quart-sized Ziploc bags and placed them in my driveway with a note taped to the top of the box that read: To whoever is taking my newspaper bags, please take this box of bags instead. The box was never taken—it sat out there for over a week (risking an HOA violation). But here's the thing, my newspaper bags have remained untouched ever since, so that's a good thing.

Ode To Dog Walkers

I don't mean to whine,
But the paper is mine.
And I don't like to squawk;
But if you've a dog to walk,
Who poops as he goes,
Then heaven knows,
Prepared you must be—
Bring a bag or two, or even three.
Because petty theft I cannot condone;
So, please leave my paper alone!

Murphy's Law ~ a universal rule, standard or regulation that dictates a customary course of conduct for forces which conspire against you in a manner that contradicts all expectations: i.e., what you don't want to happen will and, conversely, what you'd like to happen won't.

Articles of Annoyance

I. Business and Commerce

    a. Cram to complete a project on time and the minute it's finished the deadline is postponed. Murphy!

    b. Wait months for responses to work inquiries and they all come in the day before you leave on vacation. Murphy!

    c. If you stand and watch a multiple-page document get pulled through the scanner, every page will go, but look away for a minute and pages get pulled through together—and the recipient never tells you, "I see you indicate a seven-page transmission, but there are only six attached." Double Murphy!

d. Throw away some old files and you will need one of them the very next week. Murphy!

e. You finally make a purchase after much deliberating and it goes on sale the next day. Murphy!

f. You book a non-refundable airline ticket and the following day you're notified of an on-line supersaver special. Murphy!

g. Discard a coupon declaring that you'll never use it only to find yourself in the issuing store shortly thereafter. Murphy!

h. Unable to locate an item in a store, you finally ask for help only to have said item pointed out right in front of you. Murphy!

II. Automotive and Technology

a. When you're already late, you get every light red. Murphy!

b. When you're in no rush at all, you sail through every light green. Murphy!

c. You finally get around that jerk on the road only to have him sit right behind you at the next red light. Murphy!

d. Your car makes a funny noise so you bring it in for service; of course, now it purrs like a kitten. Murphy!

e. You're running late to the airport so, of course, your flight is on time; but arrive a little extra early and your flight is delayed, giving you even more time to hang out at the gate. Murphy!

f. You're waiting for an important phone call, but you have to go to the bathroom. The minute you sit down the phone rings. Murphy!

g. Just as you're making a phone call, Call Waiting beeps in. Murphy!

h. Bring your phone to the couch while watching TV and it will not ring, but leave it in the kitchen and it rings every time. Murphy!

i. Lie down to take a nap and the phone will ring. Murphy!

III. Leisure and Entertainment

a. You play Solitaire to kill time and win the first game. Murphy!

b. You get up early every day—whether you have to or not—but on the day you *must* be up early, you oversleep. Murphy!

c. You struggle to get your kids up for school, but on a Saturday, they're up at 6:00 a.m. raring to go. Murphy!

d. You almost always have an umbrella with you, but the one day you don't, naturally, it rains. Murphy!

e. Routine weekends come and go but then you get invited to two events on the same day. Murphy!

f. Dinner's on time and your guests are late; guests are on time, dinner isn't ready. Murphy!

g. You'd like the refrigerator door to stay open while you're putting away groceries, but it constantly closes; yet, reach in for one thing, expecting it to close behind you, and it stays wide open. Murphy!

h. When doing a Word Search, if you start at the top, the word you're looking for will be at the bottom; but start at the bottom and that word is hiding at the top. Murphy!

i. Ideas come to you when you're without any means to record them and when you do get the opportunity to write them down, you can't remember a single thing. Murphy!

j. Tell someone repeatedly about a funny show they just have to watch and when they finally do, the episode is a clunker. Murphy!

Ode To Murphy

What would we do without you?
You're reliable, dependable, steadfast and true.

We can count on you, time after time,
To aggravate us as you mess with our minds.

We expect one thing, yet another will happen—
That's just how it is and consistently has been.

I don't like to be petty, I don't want to complain—
But it gets on my nerves and drives me insane!

I'd like to turn the tide, if only I could...
And if it were possible, believe me, I would.

I'd like to get you—just once—for a change.
I know this vendetta may sound kind of strange.

And, of course, I'm aware that this simply can't be,
So I'll just grit my teeth and curse you, *Murphy!*

WHAT MATTERS 〜

I shouldn't let the inevitable instances of Murphy's Law aggravate me. I know there isn't anything I can do about it—it's just one of those things. What frustrates me even more, though, is I feel like an easy mark, reacting in the same fashion nearly every time with such a short fuse. I need to relax. Oh, to be one of those people who simply go with the flow.

The way I get worked up over these petty occurrences is actually contradictory to my personality. I generally have a handle on what's important in life and tend to be pretty even-tempered.

In *The Butterscotch Chronicles*, my humorous take on the ill-effects of an aging body, I put forth that none of the physical shortcomings we encounter as we make our way down the road of life really matters. In fact, much of what we occupy our time with doesn't matter.

We live our lives juggling distractions, bouncing like a pinball from one thing to another.

What truly matters, what has depth, what will last is love. As I recorded in *Butterscotch*, Frank Sinatra crooned that love is a many splendored thing. And he wasn't the only one. Many others covered this timeless classic. But for me, although love may be splendored, the word itself is just a tad overused. Disagree?

What Matters

There are songs that we love,
And movies and books.
Some love to dine out,
While some love to cook.

Some love food spicy,
Some tart or sweet.
Others love veggies,
Still others love meat.

Some love things salty,
Others love sweet,

Some love the cold,
And some love the heat.

There are those who love puzzles,
And those who love games.
Some love watching TV,
Some read when it rains.

Some love sports,
In fact, many do.
They love the game,
And the players, too.

Some love to exercise,
Some love to relax.
Some love trivia,
Supported by facts.

Some love to window-shop,
Some love to buy.
Some love the train,
And some love to fly.

Some love to travel,
Some love to stay home.
Some love to text,
Some talk on the phone.

Some love their pets,
While some love their toys.
Some love the quiet,
And some love the noise.

Some love poetry,
Others love prose.
Some love the daisy,
And some love the rose.

Love's different for everyone,
That's plain to see.
It's different for you,
And it's different for me.

There's conditional love
That comes with its strings,
But it's untethered love
That's the best of all things.

Love makes you sing,
And love makes you dance.
Let love fill your heart,
Let's give love a chance.

True love's all that matters,
In the grand scheme of things.
There's a difference it makes,
In the joy that it brings.

So let's be kind,
And love one another.
Father, mother,
Sister, brother.

What you've done in the end,
Whether big, whether small,
If not for love,
It won't matter at all.

A PITCH FOR CIVILITY ∿

So now you understand where I'm coming from with regard to love. Even though the word may be overused, unquestionably, it is positively all that matters. In fact, according to the mop-topped Fab Four, it's all you need. And wouldn't it be nice if people treated their fellow human beings this way? Or, if not with love, at the very least with a dignified respect for one another? Or is that a pie-in-the-sky unrealistic fantasy? At the risk of sounding cynical, I think it is. Somewhere along the line, the gold seems to have tarnished on that age-old sagacious rule.

So, if we can't treat others with love, or the way we'd like to be treated, how about we try—at a minimum—to at least be polite? You wouldn't think this is an unattainable goal, but it certainly seems as if it is. It appears all social decorum has eroded with the passing of time. I blame social media.

It used to be if you had an issue or something to say to someone, you'd have to confront them. It took a certain amount of bravery to address them directly, state your case, hear their reply and determine where you went from there. Sadly, those days are over.

In much the same way as a bully picks on someone smaller and weaker than themselves—who is defenseless—in order to feel bold, we've birthed an entire population of cyberbullies in this modern age. The difference is these folks happen to be small and weak themselves, but they hide behind their keyboards and cryptic user names, spouting all types of vitriol, feeling a false sense of bravado, as they hurt and destroy others with nasty posts, scathing reviews and the propagation of lies. In most of these instances, the victims have no opportunity to defend themselves with a response. Just like the bully in middle school, these anonymous posters are cowards.

A Pitch for Civility

If you don't have anything nice to say,
Turn the other cheek and walk away.

Differences of opinion are good to debate;
But not anonymously, and full of hate.

Offer your thoughts, express your view;
That's what the educated generally do.

Words are strong and full of might—
Especially when they aren't right.

False claims aired on cyberposts
And personal attacks hurt the most.

When typing on line, don't be a fool—
Keep in mind the Golden Rule.

Don't become a computer culprit.
Shut down the bully pulpit!

Scottsdale Summertime Sizzle 〜

Shortly after I moved to Arizona, I came across an article about unmistakable signs which indicate you are a fill-in-the-blank here. It was along the lines of "you know you're a redneck if...," that type of thing, but this had to do with what state you hail from. For example, you know you're from Mississippi if you call sneakers tennis shoes. Or, if you're from certain states, you'll call bubbly beverages soda while others will say pop. However, if you're from Georgia, you'll say Coke no matter what type of soda it is. When you hear someone order an orange Coke, you can be certain that person is a Georgia peach.

With my curiosity piqued, I scrolled directly to the New Jersey section first. Having lived there for 39 years—and used to Jersey (not Joisey) getting a bad rap—I couldn't help but wonder what they had to say. Now I don't remember the complete list, but I do recall thinking that they nailed it. A few of the undisputed items that stood out were:

~ When someone asks you where you're from, you give them an exit number.

~ The amusement park in Jackson is Great Adventure. It will always be Great Adventure, never Six Flags.

~ You know jughandles have nothing to do with jugs.

~ Wawa. It is a convenience store... not a condescending cry.

~ Pork Roll is a breakfast staple. And lunch. And dinner.

~ You can get French fries with gravy 24/7 since you live in the diner capital of the world.

~ The middle finger is only facetiously the state bird. The real one is the Eastern Goldfinch.

I can't imagine anyone from my old home state not wholeheartedly agreeing with all of these. Seeing as the article accurately depicted New Jersey, I scrolled back up the list to check out what they had to say about my new home state of Arizona. Again, I don't remember the complete list. At the time, I'm not even sure I fully embraced the items on the list, but I can tell you that I came to appreciate more than a few of them, like:

~ You carry a bottle of water with you everywhere you go.

~ When parking, you look for any amount of shade—even if you have to walk across the entire parking lot to get it.

~ When left out in the sun, a car's interior becomes a dangerously brutal place. Seatbelt buckles will burn you, and until the air cools things off, you must steer using only your fingertips.

~ There is no such thing as cold tap water in summer—and hose water is scalding.

~ It's not hot until the temperature exceeds 105°.

~ Flip-flops can be dress shoes.

~ You take a sweater with you wherever you go because, in most places, the A/C temps feel like sub-zero.

As I became immersed in desert living, it only seemed befitting to honor it with verse.

Scottsdale Summertime Sizzle

All over the country
The summer's begun;
Everyone's engaged,
Having fun in the sun.

But it's different for us,
Our summer's extreme;
We hide from the rays
Of the sun's scorching beam.

The snowbirds can't take it—
They leave during May.

As the mercury rises,
The heat drives them away.

The sun rises early...
Triple digits—the norm.
Out in the desert,
It's exceptionally warm.

"But it's a dry heat," they say.
Don't believe that big lie.
During monsoon,
Our humidity's high.

I've often wondered,
With our intense heat,
Could we actually fry
An egg on the street?

It wouldn't surprise me;
Things here get quite hot—
Like the inside of your car
When parked out in a lot.

Metal will burn you;
So watch that seatbelt...
If you leave something inside,
It will definitely melt!

Do not clasp the wheel,
Or your skin you will sear.
Guide with your pinkies,
That's how we steer.

And when watering plants,
Everyone knows,
The water is *hot*
When it comes from the hose.

Speaking of water,
Go nowhere without it;
Or risk dehydration,
There's no doubt about it.

The desert is rugged—
A harsh place to be,
If not for the comfort
Of good ol' A/C.

All around town
Thermostats are set low,
So you must bring a sweater
Wherever you go.

This is no joke,
I'm certainly not teasing;
I tell you the truth,
Places are freezing.

To combat the heat,
It's what we must do;
Until fall comes our way,
And summer is through.

When the rest of the country
Heads back inside,
We'll pay no attention...
We're staying outside.

Most of the year
Our weather's quite lovely,
And there's no place else
Where I'd rather be.

Unhappy Feet ~

I've been told I march to the beat of my own drum... or different drum, doesn't matter, I don't disagree. I wouldn't say I'm weird or strange, but I am definitely quirky—I recognize that. Don't we all walk to our own beat, though? I think the drumbeats vary depending on the day and who's doing the walking.

Salespeople pound the pavement. Cops walk a beat. Perpetrators don't hang around, they beat a retreat. There are those with cold feet who hotfoot it away from whatever it is they may be fleeing.

Busy go-getters don't tarry; they hit the road, make tracks or shuffle off—be it to Buffalo or any other place. Some city slickers shun taxicabs, Uber and Lyft choosing instead to hoof it across town.

The proud strut their stuff, the confident swagger, the carefree sashay and those with nowhere to go and in no rush to get there simply mosey onward. Some will stop and smell the roses as they saunter through life and others will casually amble along with an air of nonchalance.

A portion of the population will walk like a man. Others will walk tall. Unfortunately some will skulk and creep. The adventurous will blaze trails and forge ahead.

Aerosmith urged us to "walk this way." Johnny Cash walked the line. Pirates forced captives to walk the plank. Yo-yo enthusiasts walk the dog—others do that literally.

Sots reel and floozies flounce. Some get a move on. And some shake a leg—or get the lead out. Actors trod boards while the footloose trip the light fantastic. Prancing about, hoofers cut a rug, get down and boogie-oogie-oogie. As a coping mechanism, some will heed Steve Winwood's advice and put on their dancing shoes and take a chance.

The one thing all these have in common is actually two things: our feet. It is impossible to stroll, strut, shuffle, sashay or saunter without feet. So why is it, then, that feet get such a bad rap? A majority opinion—barring the odd bird with a foot fetish—is that feet are disgusting. I don't believe this, but I have an idea why it may be, and the answer could lie in all the things that go wrong with our feet.

I have an entire section dedicated to feet in *The Butterscotch Chronicles*, my anecdotal look at the impact of aging. Of all the parts that suffer wear and tear, it's our feet that take a beating. I wrote "Unhappy Feet" to close out that particular chapter.

Unhappy Feet

Athlete's Foot is the least of the woes,
That afflict our poor feet and ten little toes.

It's a fungus that grows from the toes to the heel,
That causes the skin to dry up, crack and peel.

As bad as that is, it can always be worse,
Fungus in the nail is a horrible curse.

The best course of action, I tell you it's true,
Is to take the nail off and just start anew.

Many other problems cause us distress,
Often our feet are a terrible mess.

From plantar warts, or worse, fasciitis,
Or the pain that comes from acute tendonitis.

With hammertoes, one can't wear a shoe,
I honestly don't know what these people do.

Corns can cause pain, as does a nail that's ingrown,
And so will a bunion—that's a bump on a bone.

Blisters are common and calluses, too,
These usually happen when shoes are brand-new.

The proof is quite clear, so the truth bears repeating,
From the day we are born, our feet take a beating.

DIGESTION CONGESTION ～

Congestion. The word itself almost inspires one to add "ugh" to the end of it, doesn't it? There are two definitions for congestion, both of which make me groan. The first is an excessive fullness in your vessels—think nasal or bronchial, and the second is to obstruct by overcrowding—think traffic. Now try and imagine these two things merging together, specifically within the upper and lower gastrointestinal tracts. Do I hear a resounding "ugh?" I thought so.

It's certainly possible, but not likely probable, that younger generations consider their GI tracts as much as the older population does. Young people just don't pay any attention to bodily functions; in fact, they act as if they're invincible and going to live forever—or, at the very least, their inevitable death is a long, long way off. I heard a preacher once correlate life's journey with a roll of toilet paper. Youth, he said, is when the roll is brand new—1,000 sheets wrapped around the cardboard spool—it seems as if it will last an eternity, and you don't think too much about it. But, just like the dwindling roll, as you age, time goes by faster and the years begin to disappear more quickly than the tissue squares, so you try to be a little more conservative, not wanting to prematurely reach the end of your roll.

I'm sure there are many differences between the young and the old, but let's just compare dietary intakes, shall we? Young people eat anything they want, whenever they want. For others, however, it becomes almost reckless to eat much past five p.m. The young live it up at Happy Hours, while seniors enjoy Early Bird specials. Kids' meals are often too small for most kids, but ideal for those who prefer to eat light. Unfortunately, some establishments are militant about who they serve the reduced portions to, so if you're over 12, you're out of luck.

I remember in the movie *Stand by Me*, the kids are asking each other if they could only have one food for the rest of their lives, what would it be, and the one boy says, "Pez." Not pizza, as one may expect, but Pez—those tiny sugar cubes ejected from the tracheal area of a novelty dispenser. No grown up would select that. But it doesn't end there. For some reason, it is not uncommon for younger people to savor spicy food. I used to love it—the hotter the better—but somewhere along the line, eating with my lips burning and eyes tearing lost its appeal. I've even changed my opinion on salsa. I no longer opt for the red sauces— anything with the suffix diablo is out—now I choose the green varieties like Salsa Verde. Red means "no" and green means "go." One last thing on spicy foods. When you're young, farts are funny—pull a finger and get a bit of relief, ha-ha. But after 40, gas is no laughing matter. It can present itself in stabbing, gut-searing pains, and in no uncertain circumstances would you dare trust a fart to alleviate any of that discomfort.

So you see, when you're older it just makes sense to eat a little lighter, stick with simple foods, nothing fancy. Leave the rich cream sauces, crunchy fried foods and the overly processed (read: items with a five-year shelf life) to those whose constitutions haven't been weakened over time. You have to make adjustments because your pathways have been overused—possibly abused, with not only food, but booze (sometimes the rhyme just comes out of me)—and just like on the highway, when things aren't moving smoothly, traffic backs up.

It should be obvious, what with all the mention of aging, that this is also a topic I addressed in *The Butterscotch Chronicles* and, just like the feet, I wrote a poem to close out its chapter.

Digestion Congestion

We are what we eat,
From our head to our feet.
The food we ingest,
Is not always the best.

Even though it might taste yummy,
Not all is good for the tummy.
Rich foods that are made to impress,
Often cause physical distress.

Our bodies are natural, our food should be too,
But it's loaded with additives, so what can we do?
Throw caution to the wind and eat what you will,
Because if you're uncomfortable, for that there's a pill.

There's Rolaids and Pepto and Maximum Zantac,
Gas-X, Mylanta and OTC Prilosec.
From Bromo seltzers and reliable Tums,
There's plenty to choose from to get the job done.

But what do you do should constipation arise?
The choices are many—should be no surprise.
The USA is big pharma's dream,
Intolerant of discomfort or so it would seem.

There's Metamucil and seeds—both chia and flax,
And colon hydrators, like Miralax,
Milk of Magnesia and Senokot, too,
No shortage of things to help one go poo.

If it will not come out, but remains at the door,
Try a suppository—that's what they're for.
An enema may be the worst case scenario,
But do what you must in order to go.

Impacted with poison, this waste is quite toxic,
It's so hard to function when one's full of SHIT!
I don't mean to complain, grumbling's not my style,
But understand why I'm cranky—once in a while.

GRIEF POEM 〜

Death is difficult. Most people don't even like talking about it. I never mind discussing it—it is inevitable, after all. I'm also completely prepared for it—all my proverbial ducks are in a row.

Some have suggested we live our whole lives in avoidance of death. I don't know if that's true. I do try to take care of myself—eat right, exercise, get a good night's sleep—but that isn't in order to avoid death, it's so I'm best able to enjoy my life while I'm here. Just makes sense. I will say, though, I second Woody Allen who said—and I'm paraphrasing—"I have nothing against death. I just don't want to be there when it happens." Who does, right? Well, I suppose there are a few masochists out there who like to suffer, but they are certainly not the norm.

I've lost both my natural parents—that's largely

what my book *Unconditional ~ A Story of Love and Loss* is about—so I've been confronted with profound loss. One of the things which adds to the heavy sorrow, at least in my view, is that when we lose someone we love—person or pet—we relive all our previous losses. When you boil it down, we just don't like anything taken away from us. This is an innate human quality so fundamental it's revealed in the earliest stages of life. The first word most children speak, following mama and dada, is *MINE!* We simply hold on to what we think is ours.

I've already mentioned that I'm a born-again believer and, as such, I have the biggest duck lined up. See, I am confident about where I'm going upon my physical death. Now here's where I get a little morbid. I often wonder what my own death will be like, and it's my desire to die well. I don't want to go out kicking and screaming, angry or full of fear. My wish is I remain lucid so I can focus on the joy that awaits me in heaven. I have a hope that is not of this world. Hope, as defined by Baker Encyclopedia of the Bible, "is an expectation or belief in the fulfillment of something desired based solely on the words and actions of God." It is not merely wishful thinking.

This is where it gets somewhat sticky, though. How do you express sympathetic condolences to a fellow believer? No matter how strong their faith, when a loved one passes, the hurt can be overwhelming. You can't say, "Well, the angels are rejoicing today." There's always a delicate balance between offering consoling words of wisdom and offending someone. This is the boat I found myself in when a dear friend of mine lost her husband.

After careful—and prayerful—consideration, I came up with the following which I entitled "Grief Poem," but, in retrospect, I probably should have called it "Hopeful Poem." She absolutely loved it, by the way.

Grief Poem

The angels rejoice,
Even though we may mourn;
Death awaits each of us,
From the day that we're born.

Down on earth, here,
God draws us near—
Showing mercy and grace,
While we live in this place.

But now separated,
We live worlds apart—
Cherishing memories
Held deep in our heart.

Accepting the loss,
For we know it's God's will—
Not changing the fact,
That we miss them still.

So we look up above,
Not being shortsighted,
Knowing that one day,
We'll be reunited.

Together again,
Fully restored—
Living in heaven,
With our dear Lord.

Two Haiku ～

Merriam-Webster defines haiku as an unrhymed verse form of Japanese origin having three lines containing five, seven and five syllables, respectively; and/or a poem in this form usually having a seasonal reference.

So, in the realm of miniatures, one might say the Japanese have done it again. Think about it. They are an island nation whose artisans are not only adept at cultivating teeny-tiny trees but, evidently, in crafting concise short verse, as well. They obviously like things small... just look what they used to do to their feet!

Apart from a few assignments in Mrs. Reed's English class of long ago, I've written only two haiku. The first was in jest, but the second was legit—and I'm pretty proud of it.

～

I am not a gym rat or an adrenaline junkie, but I do exercise. I hike a fair amount and I swim—three days a week for each. And although I've hiked the Grand Canyon several times—rim to rim, as a matter of fact—most of my hikes are really just what one friend once described as nothing more than walking outdoors... with a nice view. I don't take any issue with that—for the most part. I like to loosen up and get the blood flowing while out in the early morning fresh air, chatting with my fellow hikers. It's sort of the same with swimming. My friend Suzanne and I exercise our lungs and tone our bodies as we leisurely swim our laps first thing in the morning. We're not setting any records—Gertrude Ederle has no competition from us—but we enjoy it.

I don't know what it is about outdoor aerobic exercise but, for some reason, it seems to increase mucus production in the throat in a way that doesn't happen when doing indoor aerobic exercises. At least it seems that way. I can't recall ever seeing anyone spit during a group spin or step class. Yet, I see it all the time on Pinnacle Peak—my regular hiking haunt.

This may come across as a gender discriminatory comment, and be that as it may, men do not think twice about hocking it up on the trail. I'm not saying women don't spit, they do—they just tend to do it secretly, when no one is around to see it (or hear it). I would say women also consider where they spit. But guys? They don't care. They just let the phlegm balls fly, landing like oysters right in the middle of the trail. These muculent globs lie in wait, much like slapstick banana peels, ready to waylay the next unsuspecting and unobservant hiker. It's not only dangerous, it's disgusting.

Suzanne and I have discussed this many times and I know she feels the same way which is why I wasn't surprised when I received her phone call one morning right after our swim. I was still on my way home when she was entering her driveway. Living on a corner lot, before pulling into her garage, she scanned the area in a brief act of reconnaissance—to assure the coast was clear—before hocking a loogie into her own yard. Just as she launched the globule, she noticed a dog walker come around the bend. Busted! Being of the female persuasion, naturally she was embarrassed—which is, of course, why she called me in a frenzied fit of laughter. Before I pulled into my own driveway, I came up with the following:

The Loogie: A Haiku for Suzannie

A lump in the throat
Garden rocks to receive it
Seen by man with dog

I was pretty pleased with myself for crafting an actual haiku. I wondered what type of grade that would have earned me back in high school. It had all the elements—three lines, correct syllabic breakdown, not necessarily seasonal but... there was mention of a garden, so it contained a hint of nature. All in all, not bad for something that came to me while driving.

～

I've mentioned I live in the desert which, as many know, is a geographical region without deciduous trees. But I also mentioned I'm originally from New Jersey, where the state tree is the mighty Red Oak. It's the wide variety of oaks and maples, among others, that make leaf-peeping such a big draw in the fall. As the summer fades, leaves shimmer gloriously in robust reds, deep oranges and warm yellows. As I reminisce about growing up back east, I do sometimes miss the fall foliage—but never the aftermath (read: raking leaves). The crisp air and dropping leaves were always a foreboding harbinger of what was to come.

I suppose it may have been cooling off out here—with a subtle touch of nostalgic familiarity to the air—when inspiration struck and I crafted the following:

The Prelude: A Haiku

Leaves waft through the air
Stately trees will soon stand bare
Winter's on the way

DESERT SNOW

Even though my move to Arizona had nothing what-soever to do with climate, one of the big draws to the Valley of the Sun is, without question, the weather. As I mentioned, we typically get about 300 days of sun-shine. Often, when looking at a five-day forecast, it is not uncommon to see headings like: Sunny, Lots of Sunshine, Abundantly Sunny, Sun with few Clouds, Very Sunny. I am not joking. The other perk, in addi-tion to the sun, is that for the majority of the year our air is dry. I was never a big fan of humidity, but I didn't realize how much I actually hated it until I moved here. Now, everywhere else I go seems damp. But I'm getting off topic.

Most are familiar with the tongue-in-cheek cave-at regarding our heat—"but it's a dry heat." In fact, it's so popular, there are even souvenir T-shirts containing this quote—it's printed right below a picture of a saguaro propping up a skeleton. Our heat can be brutal—triple digits throughout the summer months. But here's the thing they don't tell you. During the summer, when the dew point rises it increases our humidity and brings on the monsoon season. You read that right, monsoon—violent squall, heavy downpour, threatening tempest (not the one in a teapot)—and it's these thunder-accompanied cloudbursts that are responsible for horrific flash flooding. See, that's the thing with our weather, it is severe: *intense* sunshine, *extreme* heat, *torrential* rain, *flash* floods, *forked* lightening... *Haboob* (you may have to look that one up). One thing about the desert, though, we don't typically get a lot of snow—or any snow, really. Flurries don't count.

Shortly after I made my move west, my sister came out for a visit. Hers was the last flight out of Philadelphia before the airport shutdown due to a winter blizzard. As we enjoyed our coffee the following morning, we clicked on *The Weather Channel* to see how things were shaping up back east. It wasn't too good. Although the storm had passed, Philly was buried! We watched in disbelief as residents of

Rittenhouse Square used garbage can lids and cookie sheets to dig out their snow-plowed-in cars. "Oh, my goodness," we said, "look at those poor bastards." Then chuckling, we added, "better them than us." Now, am I proud of that non-compassionate response? No, of course not; but don't worry, karma has a way of righting these things... and she is patient. Fifteen years after this episode, I finally received my comeuppance.

Snow in the desert is rare—and as I said, flurries don't even count—but it is not something that *never* happens. Sometimes snow is visible on the tops of the surrounding mountains—especially on those to the north. Even at my house, I have had two or three snowfalls which were more than just a heavy dusting—actually enough to cover the ground—but since there wasn't any real accumulation, the minute the sun came up, it erased all evidence of its existence. Why would the next snow be any different?

It was the middle of February 2019 and, just like a child, I oohed and aahed with the falling of snowflakes. To me, it's almost mesmerizing to look into the sky and see nothing but white glistening sparkles as far as the eye can see. And its rarity makes it even more wondrous, somehow. So, this particular day, a light dusting had formed in my courtyard before I went out for the evening. I drove just a couple of miles west before the flurries turned to rain. So you know what they say, right? Out of sight, out of mind.

After a nice dinner and some friendly socializing, it came time to go home. Ugh, still raining. As I made my way north, then east, halfway up Dynamite Blvd, the rain turned into a slushy mix with giant wet flakes. Those flakes took me by surprise and I began to wonder if it had been snowing at my house the whole time I was gone. I didn't have to wonder too long because very quickly the mix turned to full-on snow. I'm talking nearly blizzard-like conditions which left me driving in tiny, almost invisible tire tracks up the *center* of a two-lane road, snow-blind. Surreal!

After pulling into my garage, I walked around the winter wonderland taking pictures. Who would believe this? Three miles south of me, it was raining. Wide-eyed, I wandered around in about three inches of snow, marveling at all the beauty. Landscape lighting obscured by snow added to the mystique. I was giddy as I called my dad to share with him my magical experience.

When I woke in the morning, even though it was

still dark, I sensed a bluish cast of light in my court-yard which caused me to wonder how much snow may still be left outside. I nearly fell over with the shock. ALL of it was out there, plus about three or four inches more! I couldn't believe my eyes. Splayed shrubs were fanned out to the ground. Tree limbs were struggling to bear the weight of the heavy burden. One of my trellises had snapped in half, leaving the jasmine buried in the middle of my walkway. My young Palo Blanco, which had been wrapped in protective cloth, was bent over like a horseshoe touching the street. The previous night's beauty became a horror show. And it was STILL snowing!

Wearing an old pair of college sweatpants, I stuffed my feet into a pair of ankle boots, preparing to go outside. Since it was still coming down in big, wet flakes, I donned a hiking windbreaker with a hood. Next, I put on a pair of garden gloves and went outside armed with a push broom and a rake.

The first thing I did was cut the snowbound cloth from my tender tree, setting it free. Then, using my hands, I shook the snow off a lot of shrub-type plants. With my rake, I knocked snow off of tree branches. Unfortunately, my hood would not stay on through this exercise and a fair amount of snow went down my back via the neck hole. My fingers were frozen at this point since the icy wetness fully saturated my gloves. After pulling the jasmine out of the way, I used the push broom to clear the walkway. Remembering my pals from Philadelphia, I couldn't help but think that payback is a... well, you know.

Chilled to the bone, I went back inside, numb—both literally and figuratively. Pinnacle Canyon looked like Norway. It was unbelievable. Even more shocking, outside of maybe a three-mile radius, no one had *any* snow.

A couple of days later I took a walk through my neighborhood and the amount of destruction was overwhelming. Broken boughs atop the tallest trees were cracked and hanging on by threads, just dangling before they would eventually succumb and fall completely. Many others were already on the ground. Brittle branches of Palo Verdes and Desert Ironwoods were no match for the weight of winter's white wonder. Piles of limbs amassed in bundles were left awaiting bulk trash pickup. A sickly sourness overcame me as I contemplated the devastation that arose from something that was so beautiful. Naturally, I did what

anyone does who is sick to their stomach, I wrote a
poem.

Desert Snow

Moisture-filled clouds and temps that are low,
Combine uniquely to create winter snow.
Earthbound flakes waft to the ground—
Delicate sprinkles fall gently down.

Decorating the landscape, blankets are formed;
While crystalline sparkles, our trees do adorn.
Each limb and node, shrouded in white,
Seduce with beauty—an amazing sight.

Once leafy arms put up a good fight,
Bearing the weight throughout the long night.
This unexpected load is just too much to bear—
Snow in the desert is certainly rare.

Snapping like twigs, weakened branches give way,
Falling asunder by the breaking of day.

Gray skies clear up and out comes the sun;
Too late for our trees, though, the damage is done.

Sticks gathered together in piles and heaps,
Bulk trash will remove them by the end of the week.
Left in the wake of a captivating seduction,
Staunch victims remind us of beautiful destruction.

WAKE UP! ～

I'm not one of those people with a big bucket list—or any bucket list, really—but for some reason, I've always wanted to go to Bermuda. I've felt drawn to it, actually. It's so quaintly picturesque, maybe that's it. Anyway, I felt very similar about Santa Barbara, CA. It always looks so beautiful when filmed for TV or movies. I especially love how the bougainvillea is often shown cascading down hillsides and over wrought-iron fencing. I imagined it to be a larger version of my beloved Stone Harbor, NJ, with manicured flower beds along boutique-lined streets near the seashore. So, a few years ago I decided to visit, taking my young niece Olivia along with me for a mini vacation.

We flew in to the local airport, which was adorable, then cabbed it to our hotel. I chose a place right in the heart of town so we'd be close to shopping and within walking distance to the beach. After quickly settling in our room, we were ready to venture out to get a lay of the land. We headed directly to the Pacific Ocean first.

We'd gone about three or four blocks when we discovered we needed to go either over or under the highway to ultimately hit the shoreline. We opted for over. We went up the inclined sidewalk, over the freeway and as we began to make our descent, we were overcome with a putrid stench that momentarily stopped us in our tracks. Not knowing what was causing the odor, we looked around before preceding down the stairs on the other side. We spotted a battered shopping cart overflowing with all sorts of paraphernalia angled up against the concrete barrier. Was the smell coming from there? It appeared to be so. Not wanting to run into its owner, we hightailed it down the other side making a mental note to stick with the south side of the overpass for the rest of the trip.

With the crossing complete, we made a beeline for the sandy surf. The street we came down funneled into the pier area. To the right we saw a weathered-looking man, whose hair was bleached-out and matted, patting down a sand sculpture that we incorrectly assumed he created. A bicycle leaned against a nearby tree, its basket filled beyond capacity. To the left, there was a small brick bathroom structure that was clearly home to the man who was camped out behind its rear, amid filthy squalor. In a matter of minutes, literally, we were confronted with a reality that directly opposed the imagined idyllic town of my dreams. And it didn't end there.

The population of vagrants was overwhelming. Throughout our long weekend, we saw those who appeared nearly comatose just lying in grassy areas that aligned the seaside walkway. More than once, we saw some rifling through garbage cans. We passed many whose smell emanated off them like cartoon stink lines. They were everywhere.

This trip fell so short of my expectations, you can't imagine. Not only was I extremely uncomfortable—especially given the fact that I was responsible for my 16-year-old niece—but I was just so disappointed. Livvy told me in spite of it all, she still had a great time.

The whole situation was emotionally disturbing. When it came time to go home, the fellow at check-out asked us how our stay was, as is their wont to do. I told him that although the hotel was lovely, I was very uncomfortable with the high population of in-digents—then snidely pointed out how they didn't include anything about that in their brochure. The nearby manager, who obviously overheard my comments, came to the counter to advise me that the town was aware of the problem (you'd have to be dead not to be), then pointed out that the homeless weren't hurting anybody. I knew they weren't hurting anybody—that wasn't the point. How people can simply look the other way and ignore what's happening around them is beyond me. There is something seriously wrong if we say it is okay for human beings to live like this.

The sad thing is this is not a problem exclusive to Santa Barbara. It's happening in cities all over our country. And not to get political—because facts are facts—but the majority of these places are run by liberal politicians. Liberals who—to the detriment of their constituents—care only about what is deemed politically correct and their own selfish ambition. I poured my moral outrage into the following poem:

Wake Up!

It's time we have an open forum.
Topic to discuss: social decorum.
How on earth have we gotten here?
The crumbling of society is what I fear.

Once prosperous, urban towns
Make me sad and bring me down.
You can pick almost any city—
What's happening now is quite a pity.

Claims of help, support and aid
Don't really help at all, I'm afraid.
Beyond tragic, it's truly a crime
What has occurred over time.

Elected officials who spout compassion
From ivory towers and gated mansions,
Full of bravado, vigor and verve,
Wouldn't go near those they serve.

Let's take a look at some liberal districts.
Problems here are not easy to fix.

Cardboard structures pass for housing.
Don't you tolerate those who are grousing!

People are free to do what they please—
Disagree and you're a bigoted sleaze.
So tent cities pop up on each street and road;
People have rights, you contemptible toad.

But this isn't normal, how can we accept this—
Folks living in squalor and smelling like piss?
With garbage and feces all around,
Should be no surprise, disease will abound.

Typhus is back in the U.S. of A.
Once eradicated, it now thrives in L.A.
Transmitted especially by bodily lice,
Carried along by the rats and the mice.

Used hypodermics are easily found,
Discarded irresponsibly all over the ground.
Loud, moral outrage is oft misdirected;
While the masses become slowly infected.

There's a big disconnect and something's amiss
When we say it's okay to live like this.
Good folks stay silent, they've nothing to say,
As society slips further into decay.

Hordes of people live without dignity,
In nooks and alleys all over the city.
How did we ever get into this boat?
We can blame those who wanted your vote.

They're concerned about you—to that they'll swear,
Along with false claims to protect earth and air.
Do as they say, obey and play nice;
Not that they're heeding their own advice.

The rules don't apply to them, you see;
But they're foisted upon both you and me.
We'd better begin to start speaking up
Or it won't end with banning straws from a cup.

Self-interest and power are all that matters—
So what if the public is living in tatters.
They seem to be happy, these folks in the slum.
Pols promise the moon if it gets the job done.

Betraying their vow to keep people protected,
They're only desire is to get re-elected.
Too long now, we've been ruled by these nitwits—
It's beyond overdue, we need some term limits.

Political ambition and ensuing destruction,
Sanctuary cities and deep state corruption,
Weaken our nation, though not perfect, still great,
We must come to our senses before it's too late.

Fresh Figs ～

I mentioned earlier that I am a middle child, one with an older sister and a younger brother. I never married, nor did I have my own children. My older sister Linda married and had her kids young. My brother Tim married and had his kids later in life. This section involves each of their youngest—both boys, my nephews Michael and Griffin. They are 18 years apart in age.

Divorced early, Linda became a single mother of two... let's just say, spirited boys who did not conform easily to obedience. Constantly pushing boundaries, they often found themselves suffering the consequences of poor choices. By the time Michael was 16 years old he had been through so many rehabilitation-type curriculums he could have very easily been a 12-step program officiator. He knew the material inside and

A Collection of Poems

out—like the back of his hand, as they say—he just couldn't apply it to his own life with any longevity.

It's truly heartbreaking to watch a loved one—especially someone with their whole life ahead of them—get gripped by addiction. I'm convinced this is one of the reasons I feel so driven to teach Sunday school. My deepest wish is to help provide children with a foundation strong enough to enable them to make good choices. After—or even amid—the lessons, I often contemporize them, making them relatable to kids. It not only makes for good discussions, but it encourages application—at least I hope so. Knowing what pitfalls lie in their path, I try and counsel them, without scaring them, about what temptations the future holds. I can't remember specifically what the topic was, but one time a child asked me to confirm that it was okay to try everything at least once. I jumped on it without hesitation telling her no, it was *not* okay. I said if she wanted to try a Brussels sprout, have at it, but stay away from poison. Drugs are poison. Most addicts will tell you they wish they never started. Nancy Reagan was really on to something with her "Just Say No" campaign.

I strayed a bit, but getting back on track, I am

123

happy to report that just after his thirtieth birthday (spent in a rehab), Michael had the breakthrough so many of us had been praying for. Instead of looking to an anonymous higher power for strength, wisdom and guidance, he chose to call on Jesus, specifically. So, after nearly twenty years of substance abuse struggling—barring a couple of hiccups—he has been clean and sober for many years. In his words, "Jesus makes all the difference." Can I get an Amen?

So, one time when visiting my nephew in Palm Springs, we (Dad & I) attended a Bible-study type small group gathering with him. It was led by a pastor and his wife who were thrilled we were there to participate. They informed the group the structure of the meeting was going to be different from the typical study/discussion type format; instead they were going to play a twenty-minute recording and we were to just sit with our eyes closed and listen. I was concerned I might nod off but, as a guest, what could I do? Naturally, I acquiesced.

The audio had soft, tinkling spa-like music in the background with a male baritone plainly stating various names of God. When it began, I felt the odds of falling asleep had surely increased, but within just a few moments I was absorbed. The deep voice resounded: All Powerful. Almighty. Alpha and Omega. Compassion. Creator. Everlasting. Faithful. Good Shepherd. Healer. Holy. I am. King of Kings. Light of the World. Lord of Lords. Mighty. Most High. Prince of Peace. Promise Keeper. Protector. Provider. Redeemer. Rescuer. Sanctifier. Savior. Shelter. The Way. The Truth. The Life. Wonderful Counselor.

As I said, the litany went on for twenty minutes (and it wasn't alphabetical) so, obviously, there were a lot more names. It was magnificent and it was profound. The names were absolute—that's what struck me the most. God isn't *one* who heals, He IS healer. He isn't *one* with power, He IS power. He isn't *one* who knows the truth, He IS truth. Each name was fully encompassing—complete. He's not "a" anything, He's "the" everything.

This experience consumed me for a while. I kept thinking about how God is so big and, conversely, we are so small. I thought about all the trivial things that have a tendency to preoccupy us—monopolizing our thoughts, stressing us out and stealing our peace. And I don't use the word "trivial" lightly. I have fallen victim to this many times myself, losing perspective and fretting over things that are only momentarily important. Think about it, as you're reading this, try and recall what situation or circumstance have you obsessed over in the past? What has dominated the focus of your attention—say, something from last year, last month or even just a few weeks ago? Was it trouble with relationships? Health? Employment? I will concede that all of these are big issues, but if we're over them now—forgetting more than we generally remember—did they really warrant all the wasted time and energy? As I pondered this, an experience from long ago popped into my mind. It was a personified correlation to all my contemplation.

So, this section clearly has more to do with Michael than Griffin, but it's an episode with Griffin that was the impetus for the poem. Here's the back story. When I moved to Scottsdale my brother's kids were very young, four and two, and while their parents were working, it was my sister-in-law's mother—their grandmother—who did the baby-sitting. Since their house was cleaned on Wednesdays, Grammy kept the children at her house all day and then cooked dinner for the family in the evening. I was always invited along. Just to digress for a moment, I reciprocated on

Tuesdays and my sister-in-law Kanna had us over on Mondays. There was nothing unusual about this to the kids—so much so that once Olivia had asked one of her playmates where they ate dinner on Tuesdays. Confused, the child hesitantly replied, "Um... at home?" We did those family dinners for nearly ten years. Anyway, it's the Wednesday dinner that is the setting for *Fresh Figs*.

Fresh Figs

When my nephew was young and still very small,
He sat in his highchair, as I recall.
Dinner was not quite ready, you see;
As we waited, we discussed the tree.

"It's filled with ripe fruit," his grandmother said;
So we went out to pick some before we were fed.
The figs were delicious—so sweet and tender;
But what happened next is what I remember.

While sharing I hadn't a fresh fig before,
G grabbed one and flung it right to the floor!

"No more for you," my sister-in-law said;
Then the kid went ballistic and came out of his head.

As the pout welled up, his lip stuck out a bit,
Then almost immediately, he had a grand fit.
He gasped and wailed as tears spilled from his eyes;
"I want a fresh fig!" he desperately cried.

His heart was broken as he repeatedly sighed,
"I want a fresh fig," and continued to cry.
Nothing else mattered, but the fig he desired—
Makes me wonder, is that how we're wired?

Oft stressed and obsessed, we travel through life,
Focused on things causing us strife.
Not getting what we want lies at the root
Of dissatisfaction, like G's pulpy fruit.

But older than Griffin, learned and wise,
I had the fig in perspective, as he wiped his eyes.
Now here's the thing—it might sound a bit odd,
But this makes me think of my relation to God.

God is so big—He sees it all;
And in His eyes, I remain small.
For I am the child and He is the father.
When I fret over things, He knows I shouldn't
bother.

What we worry about will cause us distress—
Often it makes us an emotional mess.
The stuff of this life, down here on earth,
Consumes us daily, almost since birth.

Our focus misguided and quite misdirected,
The way of this world has us infected.
We're robbed of true joy as we're chasing the wind;
Because, really, it's *all*... fresh figs to Him.

Swim Time With Suzanne ～

The last time I hiked the Grand Canyon I destroyed my knees (note the plural because it was both of them). I wonder if I should have written *fourth* time as opposed to *last* time. Technically, it was the fourth time I'd traversed that massive hole (I know, it's a world wonder... to-may-to, to-mah-to). It's quite possible, though, I may never do it again; so, I suppose it may have very well been my last time. Hmm. Well, in any event, with my knees out of commission—probably needless to say—I had to lay off hiking for a while.

When I was once again ambulatory, but not quite ready for mountains, Suzanne invited me to swim with her at her gated community's clubhouse pool. She thought it would be a good source of exercise and not too taxing on my knees. As truthful as that may have been, I declined.

As a child, I loved the pool. With a pool in our backyard, I'd spend entire summers in a swimsuit—swimming from breakfast to lunch to dinner and right on through to sunset, getting out only when instructed to do so, with blue lips, chattering teeth and shriveled skin. But that, as the saying goes, was then. For some reason, as an adult, the pool lost all its appeal.

Suzanne did not stop asking me over—nor was she going to—so I finally gave in and agreed to meet her. We began swimming together one sunny Fourth of July. Now you might be thinking that swimming in the desert heat must be the most refreshing thing one can experience, and in a way it is, but that changes drastically the minute you step out of the water. With high temperatures and low humidity, as the water evaporates off your skin, it depletes your body heat, so even if it's 110 out, until all the water is completely dried off, you shake and shiver like it's freezing. It's fairly bizarre.

Anyway, turned out Suzanne was right—it was good exercise and it wasn't too hard on my knees. We began swimming together three days a week. July whizzed by, then August, and as we slipped into September, the morning air began to take on that autumn chill which so many of us out here generally look forward to, but now, due to my new routine, I was missing the torrid temps of summer.

As the third quarter of the year was coming to a close, I began to wonder how much longer I could continue to swim. Yes, the pool is heated, but with overnight lows drastically dropping, the water did not feel warm. Seeing as swimming had become a habit I surprisingly enjoyed, I did not want to stop. Hoping to minimize the chill factor, I bought a lightweight wet suit to help me endure the plummeting temperatures. I have to tell you, between this thing and my Speedo swim cap, I look like some kind of a cartoon character—not that anyone's around to see at that hour.

As October gave way to November, and mornings grew darker still, our doubts about sticking with swimming increased, but we agreed to keep at it until we just couldn't take it anymore—and then the most amazing thing happened. As the air continued to cool, the pool began to feel like bath water. We loved it!

The atmosphere of swimming this time of year is otherworldly—no longer nighttime, yet not quite day. We swim under starlit skies, while ensconced in a womb-like warmth, amid crisp clean air. Sometimes a misty fog rises off the surface of the water making it truly mystical—no wonder winter became our favorite time to swim. In spite of our embracing enthusiasm, however, there remains a bit of dread when getting out of the pool. Think about it. If you shiver in July, imagine when it's only 38 out. Brrr. But see, that's the thing. We don't think about it—you can't. You just have to get out, wrap yourself in a robe and hightail it into the clubhouse. After drying off, I slip into a fuzzy fleece, hop into my car, click on the heated seat, sip hot coffee from my awaiting Hydro Flask and ride home with a fully earned sense of accomplishment, ready to tackle my day. Friends think we're crazy. In our defense, Suzanne likes to point out how Katherine Hepburn said things like this build character. She's not wrong, either... but then again, that may just be the endorphins talking.

As winter waned and spring drew near, the mornings grew lighter with each passing day. The moon and stars were replaced with pastel skies streaked by wispy, cotton-like clouds. Chirping birds began to serenade us and desert flowers bloomed around us. Before long it would be summer again. It's remarkable how each season offers its own delight. After much discussion about it, Suzanne suggested I write a poem.

Swim Time With Suzanne

Exercise is the reason we get up and get going—
It's important, you know, to keep the blood flowing.
Seasons will come and seasons will go,
Some will bring sunshine, some will bring snow.

Early in summer, the sun is up high—
While cottony clouds adorn the sky.
Since the air is warm and the water's cool,
We ease right in to the refreshing pool.

With the coming of fall, morning light grows dim,
But that does not stop us, we still swim.
Autumn air is crisp, I tell you, it's true,
And the sky's streaked with wisps of pink amid blue.

As winter rolls 'round, there's a nip in the air,
But we pay no mind—we just don't care.

With me in my supersuit and Suzanne in her fins,
We waste no time, we jump right in.

It's a shock to the body, have no doubt,
So we don't dilly-dally before splashing about.
Wearing our bathing caps, we begin to do laps,
And when we are done, in our robes we do wrap.

Morning in winter is as dark as the night,
But the moon and the stars give us some light.
The air is quite cold, but the water is warm,
So a misty fog is sometimes formed.

Swimming in winter sure takes some guts—
If you ask our friends, they'll tell you we're nuts!
It's character-building, per Katharine Hepburn;
And she was sure right, as we've come to learn.

So even though folks think we're out of our minds,
Swimming in winter is our favorite time.
The pride of accomplishment cannot be beat—
Nor the post-swim coffee and heated seat!

Time keeps on moving and winter gives way
To the season of spring and bright, sunny days.
No longer dark, celestial orbs in retreat;
With the rising sun, the morning we greet.

Swimming is awesome by any measure,
And the shifting seasons alter our pleasure.
From starlit skies and a bright full moon
To the beauty of desert cacti in bloom.

Creation's amazing—mere words can't compare
To how it enhances the fresh morning air.
With water around us, we swim to stay fit—
But swimming with my friend is the best part of it!

CORNERSTONE GUN CLUB ⟋

Before I was born-again, I was Lutheran. For many years I attended Holy Cross church, which was presided over by Pastor Holmin. One man. When I moved west, as I mentioned, I got involved in the local church, which was a non-denominational Bible-teaching church with contemporary Christian music. In comparison, what was unusual to me, other than the dispensing of pomp and circumstance, was that they had multiple teaching pastors. That's what they called those who delivered the sermons. There were four of them on rotation. Often people would discuss who their favorites were—each had his own particular style so I suppose that makes sense. The other topic of discussion revolved around who was considered to be the heir apparent in the event the lead pastor retired.

Not surprisingly, there was a general consensus about who this person was.

So, with the unsubstantiated, commonly held belief that Pastor Jason would one day take the helm, you can imagine what a shock it was when he announced he was stepping down. To say the news rocked our church would be an understatement. Collectively, we were stunned. Stepping down? Why? Where's he going? What will he do? The answers were rather simple. Why? He felt called to go. Where? Nowhere; he was staying in Scottsdale. What will he do? Plant his own church. Wow! This would be no easy task—a divine calling is not enough. Even with God's hand upon someone, it still takes *a lot* of support to plant a church; but being so well-liked, Jason had plenty of that.

When a church is brand-new everything needs to be set up—the complete infrastructure. Many of us were eager to help Jason, and his wife Jill, in their new endeavor. Naturally, I volunteered to assist in the Kids' Ministry. And my folks were among a few couples involved in establishing the senior group, which was called Cornerstone.

As the fledgling church thrived, it was becoming

a little too difficult for my parents to remain as active as they were initially because my mother's health had begun to deteriorate. As a result, I would often accompany them to planned events so they could still participate. This enabled Dad to fulfill some of the duties required, while I looked after Mom. They were a spry and lively group. I liked them. I liked them a lot.

It had been nearly a year after my mother's passing when Fred, the founder of Cornerstone, had a new direction for the group. His vision was to have subgroups which people would engage in, within Cornerstone, thusly called Engage Groups. The idea was to expand the ministry by creating these mini communities—which would be open to any who shared a common interest—based on things that people were currently doing. For example, Book Club. This is already a popular gathering for many people, so why not have it in a church group? This would be a great way to introduce newcomers to our church. Fred was enthusiastically sharing his concept with us over dinner one night, and once we agreed his idea had merit, he buttoned up his pitch telling Dad, and I quote, "Ray, I want you to run a gun club." A few speechless moments transpired before he pointed at me and added, "And I want you to help him."

My father is an avid shooter. He and Fred, along with Fred's wife Wendy, shot together frequently. In fact, when Wendy was a nervous beginner, it was my dad who calmed her nerves and gently instructed her. I'm sure this was the motivation behind Fred's proposition. Be that as it may, once Dad recovered from the bombshell dropped by his friend, he responded matter-of-factly, "Fred, you're out of your mind!"

Fred continued to defend his position when Dad cut him off. "You've got to be kidding me, a *gun* club... in a *church*? Whoever heard of such a thing? Is Jason onboard with this?" He was. Adding my two cents, I said, "Dad, I'll help you. How hard can it be? We'll probably have six people, including the four of us. It's not a big deal." Fred was happy to hear it.

In addition to the gun club, Fred managed to pull together about a dozen other Engage Groups which were to be introduced at the next Cornerstone potluck. Before dinner, Fred explained how each group would have twenty minutes or so to discuss their respective clubs. A schedule was posted identifying which group would be in what room and the time slot we each had. As it turned out we had the last time slot, in room seven, following the book club.

As our time drew near, I went ahead of Dad to our room—which was still jam-packed with the book club. Or so I thought. I spotted Fred and Wendy among the mob. Silently, and with palms up, I shrugged my shoulders to convey my confusion. Fred responded with a smirk and arched eyebrows. It was time for words. Raising my voice over the din of the crowd, I said, "Fred, it's our time slot. Why is the book club still in here?" Smiling—like the cat who swallowed the canary—he flatly replied, "The book club is gone; we're all here for the gun club." Gulp. I ran out to get Dad.

Right out of the gate we had nearly four dozen on our roster—the majority of which were seniors, and half were women. Dad was blown away by the turn-out. Many had never shot before so we started off very slowly. We booked some space at a local gun facility and our first meeting was like a little seminar. Dad had help from many of his regular shooting buddies who took leadership roles in instruction. They, along with Dad, became our lane officers. In our first actual shoot, we rented out the facility's eight-lane Tac Bay. Having an officer with three shooters each, per lane, we had

32 participants. Needless to say, this was a far cry from the six we originally anticipated.

Over time, some have dropped out and others have joined us. Seems we always have about 42 on the roster with about 28-32 per event. We have a dependable core group. We meet once a month and, in addition to our regular shooting, I have taken to arranging small target-themed contests. Afterward, we all convene at K. O'Donnell's—the local bar and grill. It's here, over food and fellowship, where I distribute favors to each of the participants and award prizes for first, second and third place—not necessarily in that order.

With my mother gone, Dad found a fulfilling purpose in teaching his club members about shooting, as did many of his lane officers. And I love helping him. Our group is diverse—mostly seniors, that's true, but men and women alike. We're comprised of Christians, Greeks, one Jewish man, for a while we even had an atheist with us. One might be surprised to find a loving sense of community within this group—amid guns and ammo, no less—but it doesn't surprise Jesus. How do I know? Because He said so. His words are recorded in John 13:35. "By this everyone will know that you are my disciples, if you love one another." Fred was on to something with his idea for this club.

After our shoots, we typically post in the Cornerstone newsletter, sharing details and pictures from our events. One of the posts included this poem:

Cornerstone Gun Club

Every month, we all get together—
Flocked in one group like birds of a feather.
Coming in from all around—
Some from up north, some from downtown.

The group is gregarious—they could not be bolder;
It's an Engage Group, you know, for 55 and much older.
Our time together is really a hoot.
At the Scottsdale Gun Club we gather to shoot.

A gun club for seniors? Sounds kind of odd...
Especially a church group formed under God.
Fellowship and instruction is just what we do,
With Ray at the helm and his lane officers, too.

Safety's a must, so we follow the rules.
In our club, we won't allow fools.
Don't misunderstand, we like to have fun;
But there's no horsing around when it comes to a gun.

After we're done, everyone goes
Across the street to dine at K.O.'s.
We laugh and talk over meals that we eat,
Looking forward to the next time we'll meet.

REFLECTIONS

Out of all God's creatures, we are the psychological ones. And, we're emotional. Thank goodness most of our life's experiences happen in stages, not all at once, but over time, in increments, giving us the ability to prepare, to think about things and get ready.

Take pregnancy, for example. Human gestation typically takes nine months. From conception to birth, the body slowly changes as the baby develops. Can you imagine what it would be like if you conceived, then—like time-lapsed photography—blew up like a balloon and moments later delivered your child? We couldn't handle that.

Our prenatal development takes nine months, yet our full maturation takes even longer. After birth, we're coddled and nurtured. We develop our basic fundamental skills, we're socialized and we're educated before being thrown out into the world—a process that takes 18 years (if you're lucky). In contrast, look at birds; as soon as the wings develop, fledglings are kicked out of the nest. Or better yet, horses. Have you ever seen the birth of a foal? In less than two minutes after coming into the world, they wander off, wobbly-legged, into the pasture. It's incredible. We're not built that way.

Even in death, as difficult as that always is, it's a little easier on those left behind if there's time to mentally prepare for it. And when the dying process goes on too long, we often offer up prayers to end the suffering. Afterward, there is comfort to be found in that mercy. But, when death happens suddenly, not only do you have to deal with the loss, but you struggle to wrap your head around how profoundly your life has been transformed. We don't deal well with immediate change.

Most things are just better handled when dealt with incrementally. We have time to brace ourselves. Think about the whole aging process. As I suggest in *The Butterscotch Chronicles*, we manage to deal with our ever-changing bodies because those changes occur one step at a time—plus, we basically know what's in store. We have an expectation of our futures based on what we've seen and what's been openly (and privately) discussed among others. We're prepared. Hair will turn gray, things will sag, hormones will decrease and... you will begin to resemble your parents.

Some people take after their parents from day one. I didn't. I resembled Jackie Coogan. My sister and brother both have adorable round faces just like my mother's father and their bodies share the same structure as my father's family. Not me. Where did I fit in? As a middle child, I was already cultivating my syndrome when my sister planted the ultimate seed— one common among siblings, for whatever reason. She told me I was adopted.

If I may sidestep for just a moment, I think adoption is wonderful. I've taught many children over the years in Sunday school and have come across quite a few who were adopted. For some, it didn't faze them one way or another. Others loved that they were adopted and celebrated their adoption days just like—and in addition to—their birthdays. But, unfortunately, from time to time, I'd come across a child who was upset by the fact they were adopted. I counseled each the same way, telling them that their adoption actually made them extra special. For the vast majority of us, we're born into families without much fuss; but the adoptive parents, they're different. Many times, they've suffered broken hearts, gone through great physical struggles and severe psychological trials just trying to conceive. I'd tell these kids to picture their folks wanting a baby more than whatever the latest craze was, but not being able to have one; and then finally being told that they would—through adoption. I'd ask them to imagine the pure joy their folks must have felt when they got that news. And I'd wrap up the conversation by pointing out, as believers in Jesus, we are all *adopted* into God's family. It never failed to make them smile.

Okay, so all of that is from my adult wisdom, but as a kid in the early '70s, I did not embrace the idea of being adopted. Now I didn't really believe I was but, as I said, my sister planted the seed so it did nag at me from time to time. Then, one day I found an old photograph of my father when he was a young boy and I couldn't believe my eyes. See, my father lost his hair very young and apart from swimming together, in all my other memories, he wore a toupee, so it's understandable why his picture surprised me. Not only did he have a full head of hair, but his hairline was my hairline—identical (cowlick and widow's peak included). It was a comfort.

Adoption fears long since subsided, as I aged, I began to physically take after my mother. I didn't see it—even with Linda calling me Mom's clone, or the fact that one year a boyfriend gave me a monogramed robe at Christmas with the initials PJ embroidered on the lapel: Pat Junior. It's not that I didn't want to look like my mother, I just didn't think I did. My mother was beautiful. When I look back at old photos, I think she looks like a '60s model. Me? Not so much. But whether or not I acknowledged the emerging likeness, it was going to happen. Stereotypes, clichés and other generally accepted beliefs exist because there is truth to them.

Most of the time, when I look at my reflection it's full frontal. Doesn't that apply to all of us—whether fixing hair, putting on makeup, flossing, whatever? We don't come at it sideways. I'm not saying I'm not familiar with my profile; it's just not the image I have in my head when I think of what I look like. So, I was a little surprised the day I chose to use the bank's drive-thru as opposed to going into the lobby as I typically did. They have cameras and viewing screens in these things now. I could already see the teller in the bank's giant picture window, did I really need him right beside my car door as well? After the perfunctory greeting, he vanished while tending to my transaction. Casually looking around as I waited, I was struck by surprise when I encountered my own profile in the screen immediately to my left. Staring directly into the face of reality, I said, "Hello, Mother." Well, they told me it was going to happen.

Looking like my mom is not a bad thing. True, I did expect to see my own face, but if it wasn't going to be mine, it might as well be hers. But it doesn't end here. You may not have had this experience yet, but you will. One day, you won't recognize the face at all!

Now, I am not a drinker. I may have, maybe, half a dozen drinks in a year—and I'm casting no moral judgment here—I generally just don't care for a lot of it. Plus, I get up very early in the morning—no harried nights for me, thank you very much. I try and eat sensibly and, as you know, I exercise. I live an early-to-bed, early-to-rise lifestyle. I should wake up fresh as a daisy, but that is not always the case. There was one early morning when I was brutally confronted with a reflection that can only be described as grotesque. It's one thing to see your mother staring back at you but it's quite another when the mirror reveals the crumpled-up, ogre-like face of a complete stranger.

During my hike, the aftershocks of horror continued to circulate throughout my brain until finally settling into lyrical verse.

Reflections

Looking back when I was small,
A mirror hung upon my wall.
Being a child, I paid it no mind;
But that would change over time.

As I grew, so did my vanity;
And thus began shallow insanity.
Obsessed with my image, I'd primp and I'd preen.
Would you expect any less from a self-absorbed teen?

Prepubescence is really the pits—
Changing hormones trigger zits!
Back to the mirror. What else could I do?
I picked and popped them. Didn't you?

Grateful when that phase soon passed,
I thanked the Lord it did not last.
Fully grown—maturing done,
I'd have *this* face for years to come.

Mirror, Mirror on my wall,
You certainly have seen it all.
Styles change, while fads come and go—
Like '80s big hair and purple eye shadow.

The trendy quirks I undertook
Would be replaced with a classic look.
So I became somewhat less bolder—
That's what happens when one gets older.

Trying to stay fit, I exercise before dawn;
And always without any cosmetics on.
I don't look much different—I tell you the truth,
Even though I've grown a little long in the tooth.

Blessed to have had a healthy complexion,
Time takes me now in a different direction.
Don't get me wrong, I won't cause a fright,
But now I'm no longer fair like Snow White.

Many before me survived this ordeal.
The rumors are true, this is actually real.
When it happened to me, I was caught by surprise.
A little dumbfounded, I doubted my eyes.

As I stood at the glass with deep circumspection,
I could hardly believe the shocking reflection.
Though slightly familiar—the hair was a mess—
What was I looking at? I could only guess.

Well, old friend, you've been 'round all my life,
But what you're showing me now is causing me strife.
I don't understand... and I ask not to combat,
But, Mirror, please tell me, just who is *that*?

THE THIEF 〜

When I first got involved in the Kids Ministry I started out with the four-year-olds. I remained in that class for four years before I was asked to move up to first grade. Initially I was reluctant to change classes. Those little toddlers are so cute but they're also sticky at that age, so I agreed to move. I taught first grade for two years when I began to feel it may have been time for a break. The thing is, as the current class was getting ready to move up to second grade, more than a few of my kids were hesitant. I couldn't imagine why. The second grade lead teacher was a man, though, and I wondered if that had something to do with it, so I asked them. It did. Pointing out how nice Mr. Carl was did little to ease their nerves, so I asked them if they'd feel better if I moved up with them. Not only was there a resounding "YES!" but most of them latched on to me in a huddled mass so, obviously, there would be no break for Miss Melissa. Two more years passed and I was asked once again to move up, this time from second grade to the combined class of third and fourth graders—or Club 34 as it was known. I didn't hesitate.

Because of all the moving up, I had many of these children in my class for three, four or even five years, as was the case for a handful of them. Together on Sundays and Wednesdays (for our midweek program), I saw these kiddos more frequently than most of their relatives. The big difference is after they moved up to fifth grade, their relatives would continue to see them—however sporadic as it may be—and I would not, not really. I'd see them around campus from time to time, but it wouldn't be the same. I loved many of these kids as if they were my nieces and nephews, but I had to let them go. I couldn't be the weirdo teacher that continued to fawn over them, after all.

My own niece and nephew, Olivia and Griffin, often accompanied me to church and to class. I remember Liv being around eight and G only six when they participated as junior helpers—that's what I called them—in my four-year-olds class. G helped set up chairs and he ran the boom box while Liv would help set up the crafts and the snacks. As helpers, I think they felt like big shots.

I did a lot with Liv and G throughout their young lives. I already told you about our weekly dinners, which lasted the better part of a decade. Monday nights we'd go for walks around their neighborhood while waiting for dinner. We'd stroll and play mental games—games like Synonyms, Opposites or I'm thinking of a *blank* that is *descriptive word here*—I liked to engage their little brains. At my house on Tuesdays, we'd play actual games after dinner. Games like SORRY! or Pachisi (with the warped die). We played with cards, too—whether it was Old Maid (my future) or Go Fish or just building a house of cards the size of my living room area rug. It was fun. We'd also frequently walk Grammy's neighborhood on Wednesdays, then after dinner I, as the word nerd, would assist them with their vocabulary words in preparation for Thursday's spelling tests.

I was really involved in their lives, more so than I was with Linda's boys. Don't get me wrong, I was around a lot for Timmy and Michael, but with Liv and G it was different. I was much older, too—Timmy was born the year I graduated high school and Michael the year after—I'm sure that makes a difference. Anyway, it wasn't just the dinners.

I traveled a lot with my brother's family, like an au pair—that was the joke, anyway. We all got along. The majority of our trips were to Disney and Tim always said they had a better time when I came along. Sitting between Liv and G in the back of the minivan, I'd entertain them as we drove across the desert. I'd always prepare a snack bag—this just adds fun to any trip. As an early bird, I'd get the kids ready in the morning. We'd tiptoe out of the darkened room and head to a breakfast nook where I'd enjoy my coffee, and they their pastries, as we discussed the events of the prior day and what we'd expect for the given day. And in the off chance tempers flared, as children do sometimes bicker, I was a great intermediary. We have many fond memories of our trips together—and an equal amount of photo albums to boot.

And it wasn't just the family vacations, either. When Tim and Kanna had to go out of town, I'd assist in the caretaking of my little chickadees. When they were very small, their grandmother would sleep over at their house, but I'd still be involved. After the four of us went to dinner somewhere, I'd make sure that when the time came, they'd get to bed without giving Grammy a hard time. I recall one time, specifically, when they resisted bedtime and kept coming out into the living room. I walked them back to their rooms and sternly told them that I would remain outside their doors until they were sleeping. Two full minutes hadn't past when Olivia called out to Griffin, instructing him to see if I was actually there. He suggested she check. This went on for a few minutes before he ultimately gave in. As he popped his head out, I greeted him, hands on hips, with a reproving, *"Hello."* His eyebrows shot upward as he turned tail and scrambled back into bed. When Liv urged him to check on my whereabouts a second time, her words fell on deaf ears. I had to stifle my laugh.

As they got slightly older, I'd often have them at my house. We always had fun together. Whether it was grocery shopping, shopping for Sunday school crafts or any errand shopping, really—Bath & Body Works, Omaha Steaks (no, barbecue spatulas are not swords), Costco, you name it. They'd help me organize the church crafts. They'd color as I did prep work for my Tuesday dinners. We'd play our games. When it was time for bed, Liv would shower while G splashed around in the garden tub. Snug in their PJs, they'd take turns wearing either my fuzzy flower slippers or the ones with the moon and stars. These would be cast aside as they jumped back and forth from my bed to the air mattress. They were supposed to take turns on the airbed, but more times than not, I'd have them both in bed with me. Livvy with her legs strapped across me like a restraining belt and G attached to me like a magnet.

One time, after some out-of-town trip, my brother came by to retrieve his children. They were very involved in their coloring and were disappointed they had to go home. As they eventually settled in the van, Tim shared with me that he was really missing them and found it a bit disheartening when they weren't eager to go home. "It's nice to know if something happened to us, they'd be very happy with you," he said somewhat melodramatically. "They were just wrapped up in their drawing," I said. He knew that was the case. He did say it made him feel good that they were comfortable, and not crying, while they were gone.

As they got older, they still often accompanied me to church. This touched my heart in a way that is nearly indescribable. Liv was about thirteen or so, which would put G at eleven. With Tim and Kanna still sleeping, they'd get themselves up and dressed early on Sunday morning. I'd swing by to pick them up in time for the first service. After big church, as we called it, they'd help me with my class. The young girls were in awe of Olivia—"She's a teenager!" they'd marvel. Griffin helped out with the tech side of things in our large-group class setting, impressing the other adult leaders in the ministry. After church, we'd go to our usual sandwich place and pick up lunch for ourselves and my parents (their grandparents), then spend time with my folks before heading home. As time went on, and they got slightly older still, we began to incorporate driving lessons into our Sunday routines. G was so little; at twelve years of age, he had to scoot up to the edge of the seat just to reach the pedals. You may be thinking this was irresponsible, but we did it at their elementary school parking lot—which was empty on a Sunday afternoon. We called it Copper Ridge Raceway. It was exciting for them, and knowing me as a rule follower who was breaking the rules, added to their excitement, I think.

Another special thing, which became tradition, was the painting of pumpkins I did for them each year.

As I mentioned early on, I painted a Spiderman pumpkin for the church fall festival. That's what started it. G wanted his own Spiderman, and so he got one. And I made Olivia a cat pumpkin. The next year, coordinating with their Halloween costumes, I painted Griffin his beloved Buzz Lightyear on a pumpkin and I made Jasmine for Olivia. Many pumpkins followed: Mickey and Minnie, Frankenstein's monster (bolts and all) and a witch (hairy wart and all), Tim Burton's Jack Skellington and The Corpse Bride. I liked to stick with themed pairs—or couples, as it were. Tom and Jerry. Fred and Wilma Flintstone. Sylvester and Tweety. One year I did a Liv-kin and a Griff-kin. To be quite frank, these were a little creepy because they looked like severed heads. I made a SpongeBob pumpkin and a King Tyson pumpkin—a Bull Mastiff of FooPets fame. One time, I branched out and did a few from The Peanuts gang—Charlie Brown, Lucy and Linus. These were accompanied by plush toys of Snoopy and Woodstock. Since the kids were getting older and outgrowing Halloween pumpkins, I decided to go out with a bang. For the last hurrah, I made pumpkins for the whole family, painting four distinct owls. Each year these pumpkins were a surprise, but after they got them, the kids would come to my house and I'd help them paint some of their own. Now even though I thought I retired my paintbrushes after the owls, when Liv went to college, I painted her one special pumpkin containing the face of her school's mascot—go Wildcats!

It was hard to believe my young niece was in college. They say time flies, especially when you're having fun. And I can tell you I had a ball with these kids, my chicklets. I couldn't possibly love them more than I do. My mother once told me even though she enjoyed her relationships with us—her grown children—she sometimes missed her babies. At the time, I didn't fully grasp what she meant, but at this point in my life, I have come to understand exactly what she meant.

One time when the whole family gathered at Grammy's I noticed a collage-type picture on her wall that I hadn't seen before. It held a variety of photos of her grandchildren throughout many stages of their young lives. In an instant I was transported back in time and I relived the moments and events depicted. It was a haunting experience.

If I have trouble letting go of kids in my Sunday school classes, can you imagine the heartache I endure with my own little cherubs, my buddies? Liv and G are grown up now—they're young adults living their lives, so I don't see them as much as I'd like. And just as my mother experienced, I sometimes miss my babies.

The Thief

I stared at the pictures that hung on the wall;
Liv and G held the pumpkins I made them for fall.
Joy and delight filled their innocent eyes—
With Minnie and Mickey, should be no surprise.

A small slice of history captured on print,
Immobilized me there, just for a bit.
With Liv around seven and G only five,
Love welled up within me and I nearly cried.

Not so long past, but a lifetime away,
They were only small children—seems like yesterday.
Time is sure fleeting, as many do say,
My young niece and nephew are full-grown today.

No more sleepovers with slippers like flowers,
No coloring, crafts or giggling for hours.

No helping with homework or vacations to Disney,
　　Or getting out of bed just a little too early.

　　The years go by and children mature;
　　　It's a natural process, that's for sure.
　And while it may be fun watching them grow,
　　　It's still tough, sometimes, just letting go.

　　But holding the wind cannot be done,
　　Nor is it possible to catch up to the sun.
　　Trying to do so defies logic and reason;
We must accept, then, there's a time for all seasons.

　So I gazed at the photos, lost in their smiles,
　　And wished to go back, if just for a while.
But I understand nature and know this can't be;
　　　Yet, I miss my sweet cherubs—
　　　　time stole them from me.

A Poem for the Rothfelds ～

You may be asking yourself, *Who are the Rothfelds?*
Heck, who could blame you? It's not as if the name car-
ries some dynastic importance like, say, the Kennedys.
It doesn't. So, who are they? They're friends of mine
and they are important to me. Mrs. Rothfeld happens
to be my friend Suzanne—or Suzannie, as I often call
her.

One of the most profound things I learned
through our friendship is that the depth of a relationship has nothing to do with the longevity of a relationship. I was in my late forties before we became friends
and we couldn't be closer.

My first introduction to Suzanne was through
the regular Pinnacle Peak hikers. She hiked different
days and times than I did, though, so, apart from the
occasional coffee klatch, our paths didn't really cross.

I simply knew her as the French girl... the one who fell in the cactus that time. It wasn't until my hiking buddy Howard told me that she attended the same church as I did that I specifically sought her out. It was during an Easter service when I finally spotted her. Hurrying down off the choir risers, I called out to her as the congregation was leaving the sanctuary. This is when I formally introduced myself and our friendship began.

One afternoon, over a glass of refreshing iced tea, we really got to know each other. The conversation began in a typical manner, sharing some basic stories about things we had in common, like hiking and our church, but then it turned, and soon we were discussing many private matters—deeply held thoughts and emotions just pouring out of both of us. I think we were equally surprised by the instant rapport. It was all very easy and natural. And it's rare.

Over the ensuing years our friendship has only grown stronger. We exercise together. We worship together. We've travelled together. I once told her she's my most stable friend—because she is. Every now and then, after doing something silly, she'll say, "I can't believe you think I'm stable." And each time I'm forced to correct her. "I never said you were stable. I said you were my most stable friend." There's a big difference. I'm not sure who this speaks more about, her or my other friends, but be that as it may. I think Alan's amused by this assertion of stability. Alan, of course, is Mr. Rothfeld.

He's another one I liked from the moment I met him, but he is quite different from Suzanne. Suzanne is easygoing, for example. Alan is a little more particular, I'd say. Suzanne is French Canadian, and Christian. Alan is a Jewish man from Brooklyn. Suzanne is active. Alan is a mouse potato. (I just learned this new slang word: a person who spends a great deal of time using a computer.) Now, even though we know opposites attract, these two are from such completely different worlds it just begs the question, how on earth did they ever get together?

When I asked, Suzanne first told me that Alan picked her up on the street. This, as it turned out, was one of those humorous statements with some truth behind it. As the story goes, Suzanne was walking down the street with a girlfriend when two American businessmen caught their eye. These brazen young men asked the two lovely ladies to join them for a drink. How this happened with the language barrier I don't exactly know. (In my mind, I picture charades.) Well, the girls took them up on it, and the rest, as they say, is history.

Alan was smitten with Suzanne and he wasted no time making his interest quite plain. While wooing her, he proposed in a love letter. Drawn to his strong, confident personality, she accepted and moved her life to New York. Eventually they made their way to Arizona.

Now here's a mindblower. Several years into our friendship, I found out that Alan's first cousin is the mother of one of my childhood friends. How bizarre is that? I mean, really, what are the odds? Someone call Kevin Bacon. What this really tells me, though, is that we were destined to be pals—or *amies*, if you'll pardon my French.

Anyway, the lovebirds have been together for many years now—and to think it all began from a chance meeting on the street. Here's what I wrote in the card for their thirty-sixth wedding anniversary:

A Poem for the Rothfelds

It all began on a Canadian street.
He saw her and thought, *Ooh, she looks sweet*.
She didn't know quite what to think;
But what's the harm in one little drink?

"I'm from Quebec City," she said. "How about you?"
He said, "I'm here on business. I'm a Brooklyn Jew."
"Really?" she replied. "What is it you do?"
"I'm in insurance and I'm into YOU!"

Who was this guy, so confident and bright?
She was drawn to him from that very first night.
Getting to know each other was such a delight,
When he said, "Marry me," she said, "All right."

So she moved to New York, then on to AZ,
Gathering each year one more anniversary.
Wed in October so long ago
Makes one wonder, where does the time go?

They've shared ups and downs, laughter and tears
Hopes and fears for thirty-six years.

Hand in hand they've faced all kinds of weather...
May they always be happy together.

Happy Birthday, Jason ～ၚ

Unlike the Rothfelds, who you had no idea of, you can, with confident accuracy, correctly assume who Jason is. He is the pastor I spoke of earlier, the one who leads Illuminate Community Church.

When delivering sermons in a way that makes them relatable, pastors often share personal information from the pulpit and, as such, you can't help but get to know them on a somewhat intimate level. Since my folks were friends with Jason's parents, I was also sometimes privy to family stories that the general congregation may not have been aware of. Plus, I had their youngest child, Faith (my precious), in my classes for three years—remember on both Sundays and Wednesdays—so I got to know even more about the family (kids really do say the darndest things). And, as you know, I was one of the many who were eager to assist him in getting his newly planted church off the ground—a privilege I'll always hold dear.

Anyway, a common claim—especially among believers—is that each one of us has been born at the particular time we were for a particular reason, in order to fulfill our part in God's plan. This thought must have occurred to Jason's mother when she found out she was, once again, with child. In her late thirties, presuming her child-rearing days were behind her, this news had to be a big shock, to say the least. But God's timing is perfect. And so, late in 1969, Jason was born.

Fifty years later, fully grown and with a family of his own, he is surrounded by love as he shepherds the flock through his God-ordained ministry. As an expression of this love, as his fiftieth birthday approached, someone bought a journal and suggested we all write birthday messages in it. I was more than happy to contribute but... what to say? What to say? It should be no surprise to you now, I came up with a poem, of course. Here's how I welcomed him to this side of the hill:

Happy Birthday, Jason

Fifty years back, as the '70s drew near;
Caught by surprise, his mom cried, "Oh, dear!"
"I didn't expect, again, to give birth..."
But late in October, Jason came to this earth.

From baby to toddler, then kid on to man—
Time quickly passed by as only time can.
Soaking up knowledge and experiencing life—
Along the way, taking Jill for his wife.

Together they had a goal to move toward,
Obediently following the path of the Lord.
In times of fear, in their faith they'd abide,
Knowing full well where God guides, He provides.

At the helm of Illuminate, you make us smile.
Planting God's seeds is certainly worthwhile.
You're truly successful, by every measure,
Storing in heaven a bountiful treasure.

Gifted to prep us for God's kingdom come,
One day He will tell you, "Good job and well done."

Until that day comes, may you continue to soar—
Happy Birthday, Jason, may you have fifty more!

THE LONGEST MONTH ~

Thirty days has September, April, June and November, all the rest have thirty-one except... except... I can never remember the rest of this mnemonic, but it doesn't matter, does it? We all know February has only 28 days, generally speaking. Okay, I looked it up. The balance of the verse goes like this: But February's twenty-eight, the leap year, which comes once in four, gives February one day more. No wonder I forgot it. Anyway, we really don't need any tricky assistance to recall how many days are in February, but the device is certainly helpful to differentiate between the 30- and 31-day months, that's for sure.

In the preface to "Scottsdale Summertime Sizzle" I mentioned how there are regional commonalities that can sometimes define who you are and where you grew up. Another key identifier may be the idioms we use. For example, you will never—if I may digress, I generally don't like using absolute words like never and always, but in this case, I feel certain the word is apropos—you will never hear someone who grew up in the city say "I was as nervous as a cat in a room full of rocking chairs." So, if you do happen to hear this come from the mouth of some urban cowboy, you can bet your bottom dollar he is originally from a rural community. Another bucolic turn of phrase which you may or may not be familiar with is *as slow as molasses in January*. Now, I did not grow up in the city, nor did I grow up the country. I grew up in a suburb; but, I did date a country boy years ago. One of the things I kept from that relationship is this quaint expression.

It paints a good word picture for slowness, doesn't it? I mean, most of us know that molasses is thick and gooey—like old honey. It doesn't quite pour from a jar but, more aptly, it oozes. And this is in the best of circumstances—throw the frigid temps of winter into the mix and its fluidity almost grinds to a complete halt. In my opinion, it's not only molasses, but time itself that screeches to a standstill in January.

The little month of February, even though it's only a couple days shy from the length of its cousins, flies by. Wouldn't you agree? It just about begins when all of a sudden you're polishing off the last of the Valentine chocolate and discarding the roses. St. Patrick's Day comes and goes, then you're knee-deep into Easter activities. Springtime bursts onto the scene and before you know it, we're celebrating moms, dads and grads. Summer launches a season of fun in the sun. We enjoy barbecues, pool parties, vacations and more. Inevitably, kids return to school and as the air cools, fall festivals are planned. Halloween passes and preparations begin for the grand holiday season. We have feasts to plan, homes to decorate, gifts to buy (and wrap), goodies to bake, festive functions to attend, holiday traditions to uphold, resolutions to set, and then... NOTHING.

Tick... tock, tick... tock. The first week of January feels about a month long. By the second week, Christmas is already a distant memory. By the beginning of the third week, you've only just crossed the halfway mark. Tick... tock, tick... tock. It's seems interminable. Here's the poem I wrote while anxiously awaiting the arrival of February—when life begins again:

The Longest Month

Summer slips easily right into fall,
With nary a notice, most don't care at all.
Caught in the hoopla of nonstop hecticity,
Completely rapt in all the festivity.

With so little time, and much to be done,
Days quickly pass by, with all of the fun.
As December wraps up and draws to its close,
It feels like a death sentence—no more ribbons or
bows.

Social calendars now empty; the parties are through.
It's back to reality. What else can one do?
Resume the routine... get your head back in the game.
This is nothing new—each year it's the same.

Time, which once sped, has come to a halt—
The function of which seems to be in default.
The year starts off slowly as we get into the grind;
Like the flow of molasses, it's the same every time.

Moaning and groaning with fits and with grunts—
It's not just the first, there are six other months.
A total of seven have of thirty-one days;
So, January's not longer, it just *feels* that way!

FEAR NOT 〜

Hoping to one day fly like an eagle, The Steve Miller Band famously informed us that time keeps on slippin' slippin' slippin' into the future. But it doesn't really, does it? It slips into the past. Minute by minute, present moments recede into history. Therefore, each day, event or occurrence is all history in the making. Some incidents are bigger than others, though. Some will stand out over time. Some will not soon be forgotten. I'm talking about the 2020 pandemic, of course.

Wise King Solomon often reminds us that there is nothing new under the sun, and that still holds true today—even for the global calamity known as COVID-19. The world has seen this type of thing before. It's experienced Black Death, Yellow Fever, Polio, Ebola, SARS, MERS, bird flu, swine flu, and the list goes on. Viruses go viral, it's what they do. However, this coronavirus is supposed to be different—novel is the word they use. Not being an epidemiologist, I don't know what makes it novel; I do believe, though, it may be the only one to launch some new vocabulary. *Shelter in place* and *social distance* are just two phrases that did not seem to exist prior to this episode.

This teeny-tiny microbe—invisible to the naked eye—turned the world upside down. And, as contagious as it may be, it's not quite as contagious as the panic it incited. As nonessential businesses were being shut down, it became an every-man-for-himself situation. Stores were ransacked and pillaged as hysteria birthed a new breed of hoarder. Third world villages may have been better off than us. We're so civilized it seems we've rendered ourselves unable to function when our lives become disrupted. People went berserk. Never once were we without our creature comforts—we had electricity, running water, climate-controlled environments—we just had to stay home. Two decades after the predicted Y2K apocalypse fizzled out, I am grateful once again for that disaster not coming to fruition. That truly would have been devastating. Our recent circumstances prove we would not have been able to survive it.

Staying home was not an issue for me. I already live a hermit-like life. And since I work from home, I never once felt isolated throughout the whole ordeal. I'm prudent, responsible and, probably because I live alone, I'm generally prepared for the unforeseen. I'm usually stocked with backup supplies—like a normal amount of things, not prepper quantities. You are not likely to ever hear me ask, "Hey, who moved my cheese?" And although I was never a Girl Scout, somehow, being prepared is ingrained in me—it is an essential part of who I am.

I've also been known to be industrious and creatively inventive. Years ago I was in a social setting with about five other couples. I don't know why our discussion turned to this topic, but the question was raised if we were to be shipwrecked, which of each pair would you want with you on the island? My poor boyfriend didn't get a single vote. Each apology came to him with the explanation that I was crafty and, therefore, the better choice. I'm not tooting my own horn here, but it could be that this aspect of my personality is what prevented me from getting delirious over toilet paper—or the lack thereof. Honestly, the mass confiscation of TP was quite a surprise.

When the suggested two-week quarantine stretched to four, then Easter came and went, with May on the horizon, I began to have some doubts about the whole thing. There was so much conflicting information and as the divide grew along political lines, one couldn't help but feel the crisis was being exploited—it couldn't go to waste, after all. Ordinances, guidelines and general suggestions had no continuity across state lines. Nothing added up. Their rules didn't make sense. With our civil liberties in jeopardy, it was as if we were living under the Gestapo. Still, as I heard about these outrageous stories, I refused to get sucked into all the madness.

I'm blessed to work at home. I live in a great climate. I exercise amid nature on beautiful open trails at the crack of dawn. All my family and loved ones are safe. I am grateful and I keep my faith in God above.

This reminds me of an old joke. A town is being evacuated because a flood is coming. A pickup passes a pastor's home and the driver calls out, telling the pastor to hop in. The pastor refuses. He says he has trust in the Lord and won't be forsaken. The pickup leaves. With the waters rising, a boat comes down the street. The rowing man calls out to the pastor who's found himself trapped on the second floor. Still the pastor refuses help, advising his would-be rescuer that he has led a faithful life in service to the Lord and would not be forsaken. The boat leaves. Now on the roof of his house, he sees a helicopter overhead. As the ladder is dropped down, the pastor denies help a third time, yelling upward that he is confident the Lord will provide for him. The helicopter leaves. The pastor drowns. When he encounters the Lord in heaven he's flabbergasted and he asks, point-blank, "How could you let me perish when I faithfully dedicated my entire life to you?" The Lord replied, "I sent a truck, a boat and a helicopter. What more did you want?" I like that joke because it has a certain poignancy, I think. Miracles don't always have to be miraculous.

I've been accused of sometimes getting a little too preachy. It doesn't bother me. I'm just sharing my thoughts, feelings and beliefs. I'm not forcing them on anybody else. I don't think I would offend anyone if I was, say, sharing a recipe for Key Lime pie—even if I was claiming it was the best recipe—but for some reason, faith strikes a chord. I wonder why that is. It's worth examining I think. In any event, my faith works for me—I have peace. Who wouldn't want that?

In one section of my book *Unconditional ~ A Story of Love and Loss*, I wrote: "Beliefs are one thing. Faith is another. The real test comes when you have to faithfully trust and believe in what you presume to be true. Do you trust God? Does He have a plan? Although there may be clarity with hindsight, heading into the storm the path is not always clear. It's when we can't see that we must remind ourselves to hold on and trust." See, you need faith in tough times, not when you're riding high.

And something else to keep in mind, nothing lasts forever. Good times don't last and bad times don't last, either. For some reason we expect stress-free good times to be the norm—I don't know why, that's pure fantasy—and it's why we end up devastated when trouble comes. But the thing is, the distressing times will only last a season also. Highs and lows, my friend—two sides of the same coin.

So when things seem out of our control—which is most of the time—I remind myself of three biblical verses to help me keep my focus on what's important. The first is from the Old Testament book of Proverbs and the others are from two of St. Paul's letters found in the New Testament. The three of them go together as one coherent thought: Trust in the Lord with all your heart and lean not on your own understanding. Set your minds on things that are above, not on things that are on the earth. And the peace of God, which surpasses all understanding, will guard your hearts and your minds in Christ Jesus.

I'm certainly not a Bible scholar—just a lay person making my way in the world—but I have heard it said that "Fear not!" is the most repeated command in the Bible. Who am I to argue?

Fear Not

COVID-19
Caused a global hysteria—
Akin to Yellow Fever
And jungle malaria.
Like Panama's Big Scare,
Not one was secure;
Anxious and waiting,
We hoped for a cure.

It was 24/7
Non-stop doom and gloom,
On every device
And in every room.
There's no situation
Which panic improves—
Except possibly the ratings
Of TV daily news.

Keep a cool head—
No fretting, don't dread.
With all the uncertainty,
That's easier said.
Flocked together,
Like birds of a feather,
Folks braced themselves
For unknown stormy weather.

But this was *not*
The doomsday hour—
Never once
Were we without power.
True, we were unable
To freely roam;

Asked, instead,
To simply stay home.

Keep your hands washed
And don't touch your face;
Practice social distancing
And shelter in place.
Asked to stay put?
Can you believe the nerve?
Would that really help
To flatten the curve?

An all-out effort
To limit those who'd get sick,
Bore a new contagion, however—
A state of heightened panic!
When logic falls away,
Thinking's not clear—
And that's the real danger
When dealing with fear.

Leaders tried their best
To be providential,

Closing up businesses
Deemed nonessential.
Cities resembled
Abandoned ghost towns,
As Governors declared
Near total lockdowns.

Groceries were flooded
As folks grabbed for themselves,
Leaving behind
Eerily empty shelves.
Like Soviet co-ops,
I tell you it's true,
Stores looked like Whoville
After the Grinch passed through.

People stocked up,
Feeling lost and dejected;
But hoarding the TP
Was quite unexpected.
Folks have so much now—
Abundantly more than their fill—
Unused rolls will be left
To heirs in a will.

The mob mentality
Stoked trepidation and fuss,
And generated more fear
Than the coronavirus.
Not to make light
Of those who did suffer,
But just like all trials,
These things make us tougher.

As time dragged on,
So grew my doubt;
Curiosity took hold:
What was this about?
Stories of hope
Were largely ignored,
Yet fear-mongering claims
Continued to soar.

Misinformation
Was put forth every hour.
Could this possibly be
About usurping power?
When two and two
Cease to be four,

One must wonder
What's really in store.

The split down the aisle
Was no big surprise,
As our rights were eroded
Before our very eyes.
Not wanting to miss out,
Libs had to make haste—
They could not risk a tragedy
Going to waste.

The threat was contained,
Our behavior was changed,
And the economy continued
To slip right down the drain.
Yet still there were those
Who wished to stay closed;
"But why?" is the question
That naturally rose.

Life has been altered,
Liberty's in regress—
We're no longer free

To pursue happiness.
They're rewriting laws,
And causing great pain,
Stimulating nothing
But political gain.

Our quality of life
Lies in the hands of a few;
And they think they know better
Than me and you.
Sounds kind of arrogant—
Can you believe the nerve?
Don't be surprised;
It's just what we deserve.

We've been disengaged,
Wrapped up in ourselves—
Our decisions now made
By political swells.
Even though they live lives
Of great contradiction;
Remember their goal:
Societal friction.

One must keep in mind
And always remember
They will discount whatever
Does not meet their agenda.
I shudder to think
That it may be too late—
As we're already living
In a near police state.

Authority's abused
In the name of public protection.
That's the big takeaway
From this viral infection.
We must do what we're told,
It's the same every time;
Or suffer penalties and fines
If we step out of line.

So, as a pawn,
I've just one question to ask:
How long must I go about
Wearing a mask?
I'd like to return
To our daily routine;

When that may happen,
Remains to be seen.

No one said it would be easy
Living this life.
Why would we expect it
To be free of all strife?
When the upsets come,
I don't cry, push or shove;
I try and stay calm,
Setting my eyes up above.

I pray for the strength
To help me endure
Whatever crosses my path
Or what might lie in store.
If our culture's in tatters
Or if I can't find a roll,
I'll rest in the fact
That God's in control.

EPILOGUE ∽ ALL GOOD THINGS

Poetry is defined as a work in which special intensity is given to the expression of feelings and ideas by the use of distinctive style and rhythm. Of course, I'm partial to the kind that rhymes.

Seriously, though, to me, poetry is in all things. Poetry in motion, as they say. Its presence can be found in the fluid rhythm of life. Like wafting banners gently billowing in a breeze, the essence of nature itself is poetic. And it's everywhere. It's the view from a mountaintop. It's the salty waves lapping at the shoreline. It's sunrises and sunsets. And blooming flowers. And singing birds. It's found in accomplishment and defeat. In elation and sadness. Birth and death.

Poetry is soul-baring. Even my little poems reveal what's truly important to me. Emotions stir my heart and thoughts form in my head, and like sand off a beach blanket or crumbs from a tablecloth, I shake them out and capture them on paper. Then I fashion them into verse. Well... it's time.

All Good Things

All good things—if I may be so bold,
Must come to an end before they get old.
So now that it's over, with all said and done,
As you read my poems, I hope you had fun.

My thoughts now recorded for posterity,
To be shared by any, whoe'er they may be.
I've opened my heart and bared it, uncovered;
Sharing my feelings, here's what's been discovered.

Special days, holidays and days without end.
Time spent with loved ones, hanging out with some
friends.
Rainy days, snow days and days full of sun;
Hiking and swimming and shooting some guns.

I don't shy away, and I have no compunction,
When it comes to discussing a bodily function.
But what matters more are affairs of the heart—
It's emotional stuff that rips us apart.

Our culture may change and manners decline;
Bodies will age with the passing of time.
We taste love and loss—yes, these things are big;
But take heart and fear not for they're only fresh figs.

Life is pure beauty—it's why the birds sing—
There's a poem to be found in most anything.
Well, this is it now, the end of our time,
I sincerely hope you enjoyed all the rhyme.

⮜ CONTACT M. HILL ⮞

Write M. Hill via her website at:
www.HoneybeePublishing.com

or email her at:
MHill.Honeybee@cox.net

BONUS FEATURE 〜 GENESIS

Each of us have our own special gifts. I'm creative, that's one of mine.

Back in my theater days, one critic wrote of my impeccable comic timing. I was flattered. But for me, it ended there. Not being able to sing or dance, I was not what they call a triple threat. I wasn't any threat at all, actually—but I had a good time playing different characters and creating entertainment for others. There's still a gifted skill in that, singular as it may be.

Some are extremely gifted in technology. Almost all of it befuddles me. I live a life that Laura Ingalls would be comfortable in. And I'm okay with that. Different strokes...

Part of my creativity gift is the knack I have for putting things together. First of all, as I mentioned, I am very organized, and I always have been. This is an innate characteristic of mine. Secondly, I'm fairly adept at figuring things out—I must get this from my mother who could have, had she chosen, been a detective. It's probably what makes me good at all the puzzles I enjoy. It's also at the root, I believe, of my ability to craft the storytelling poems you just read.

Anyway, along these lines, I decided to include the following piece—written years ago—simply for your enjoyment. It's a demonstrative example of how I can put things together.

IN THE BEGINNING a few classmates got together and formed a band. Over four decades later that band finally received the long overdue recognition that loyal fans always knew they deserved. On March 15, 2010, Genesis was inducted into the Rock and Roll Hall of Fame.

I first became a fan, as a teenager, back in the early '80s with the release of *Abacab*. I actually won that album at a boardwalk game of chance at the Jersey shore and that, as it turned out, was just the beginning.

Their music spoke to me—the melodies,

the stories—and I just couldn't get enough. They became a hobby of mine. I got all their past albums, interview records, picture books, you name it—if it could be had, I got a hold of it. I spent hours admiring album cover artwork and digesting lyrics while listening to these guys.

Killing time one day back in 1987, from memory, I jotted down a list of all their albums in the order in which they were released. I then decided to see if I could write down the titles of all the songs on each album—I couldn't do this today, not by a long shot, but I could back then; these were my boys and I loved everything about them. With the list before me, I wondered how many song titles I could use in writing one little story.

What you'll read below is the fruit of my labor, a fictitious letter to a fictitious cousin—song titles italicized...

Dear Cousin,
What's up? *It* is I again. How are you?

I'm fine. Have you see any good movies lately? I did. The other night *Me and Sarah Jane* and *Harold the Barrel* went to *The Cinema Show*. There was a double feature—*Return of the Giant Hogweed* and a mystery called *Who Dunnit?* After that we stopped at *The Fountain of Salmacis* for a while. Typically, Harold had *Many Too Many* drinks and began reciting the *Ballad of Big*; but at least he didn't sing that Boy Scout *Fireside Song* like he usually does. Sarah wasn't much help either. She spent the whole night *Looking for Someone*. It wasn't too bad, though, *Me and Virgil*, the bartender, had a nice conversation. *Please Don't Ask* me how I get into these situations.

I was sorry to hear that you've been *Down and Out* because your girlfriend broke up with you—but don't limit yourself, broaden your *Horizons*. *Like It or Not*, I've got to tell you that acting like the lonely *Man on the Corner* isn't going to help matters at all—you're *Taking It All Too Hard*. *It's Gonna Get Better* once you realize that *The Lady Lies!*

Your *Mama* always said that you have *Your Own Special Way*, so stop *Throwing It All Away* on everything and *Anything She Does*. True, you may be hurting right now, but *Keep It Dark*—after all, you're a *Man of our Times*. Don't let her keep you *In Limbo* forever. *Am I Very Wrong* for telling you this? I hope not. You know *One Day* you'll find the girl of your dreams.

Hey, did you hear we're moving? Now we have to *Get 'em Out By Friday*. We bought a *Home by the Sea*—it's our *Second Home by the Sea*, actually. This one is the center house in a *Cul-de-Sac*. I still won't go swimming, though, not since that incident with the *Undertow*—you remember. I suppose I don't really mind moving. *Back in New York City* there are constant incidents of *Robbery, Assault and Battery*—that town is like a *Land of Confusion!* But still, I'm sure I'll miss the *Broadway Melody* that you can sometimes hear during *Twilight* as *The Light Dies Down on Broadway*. I don't know, I just wish I had *A Place to Call My Own*. Do you ever miss the city now that you live out *In the Wilderness?*

Oh, remember the *Illegal Alien* I wrote you about, you know, *The Brazilian?* Well, we went out again and he gave me another gift—this time it was a *Musical Box.* Do you think I'm getting *In Too Deep?* Last week we went to that new club, *For Absent Friends,* and I felt like I was *Dancing with a Moonlit Knight.* Then later, while walking home *In the Glow of the Night,* I could swear I saw a *Silver Rainbow!* You know how it is with me, *Entangled* in romance—*More Fool Me!* Did I tell you he calls me *Duchess?* I don't know, though. *In the Beginning* when he asked me about my feelings, I gave him *No Reply at All.* But he's like *The Conqueror*—he's got some sort of *Invisible Touch* on me. Yet, I'm just not sure, I mean, *I Know What I Like,* but, well, *You Might Recall* what happened *After the Ordeal* with *The Eleventh Earl of Mar.* I don't want this relationship to be overcome with *Stagnation* just as *The Sour Turns to Sweet.* Perhaps I should stop trying to read

Behind the Lines—that type of thing could create a *Misunderstanding*. I just don't know what to do. That's why I'm *Alone Tonight* writing to you instead of going out. Forget dating casually, that whole scenario is typically *All in a Mouse's Night, Just a Job To Do*, really, *That's All* it is. On the other hand, sometimes I feel as though I'm stuck in *The Waiting Room* of some sort of *Chamber of 32 Doors*, meandering up and down each *Aisle of Plenty, Counting Out Time*, trying to avoid *The Serpent* while looking for that *One for the Vine*. But who am I kidding? What's really out there is nothing more than a *Grand Parade of Lifeless Packaging*—a bunch of *Dodo/Lurker* types. Maybe it's all part of some big plan, or maybe it's just a *Trick of the Tail*, who knows? But enough of that!

Thanks for those *Harlequin* romance books you sent me. I agree with you—*Visions of Angels* is definitely better than *Scenes from a Night's Dream*. Thanks again! Hey, what did you think of Uncle *Duke's Travels*? I can't believe that he actually climbed to the top of *White Mountain!* What's really unbelievable, though, is *The Knife* he found that supposedly dates back to *The Battle of Epping Forest!* Oh, and you should see the necklace he brought back for me—it has *Seven Stones* in it. It's gorgeous!

I was listening to *Unquiet Slumbers for the Sleepers in That Quiet Earth* by Genesis. Have you ever heard of them? *Anyway*, it just ended so let me go *Turn It On Again*... I'm back. I decided to *Put Another Record On* instead, so now I'm listening to *Abacab*.

I'm just noticing from looking out my *Window* that it's nearly *Dusk* and amidst the *Afterglow* of the setting *Silent Sun, Mad Man Moon* can faintly be seen while the breath from the *Watcher of the Skies* gently creates *Ripples* that glide across the sweet, pink water of our pool. Who can deny the *Evidence of Autumn?*

Well, cuz, I've got to go, *Supper's Ready*. We're having *Domino*'s pizza. Don't stay *In Hiding*—keep in touch. *Los Endos.*

Love always, *Lilywhite Lilith*

P.S. Did you hear about my new pet?
I actually got a *Squonk!* I heard you got a...
Wot, Gorilla? That's a little hard to believe!

That letter used 106 song titles from 14 albums. So, okay, I obviously had a lot of time to kill back then. Plus, as I've been known to say, what's the point of having a disorder if you're not going to be obsessive and compulsive about it?

I'll let some other crazed fan write the return response using post-1987 song titles and the earlier ones I didn't use—I just don't have that kind of time anymore. But make no mistake, even though the amount of free time I have may have diminished, my fondness for the band from my youth has not. And so, let me say congrats to the boys—they've come a long way since playing Upstairs at Ronnie's. Genesis—a musical REVELATION. ☺

CPSIA information can be obtained
at www.ICGtesting.com
Printed in the USA
LVHW010849300920
667476LV00004B/264